STATE ART COLLECTION   ART GALLERY OF WEST

State Art Collection
Art Gallery of Western Australia

Published by the Art Gallery of Western Australia

Copyright © 1997
Art Gallery of Western Australia
All rights reserved

This book is copyright. Apart from any fair dealing for the purpose
of private research, criticism or review, as permitted under the
Copyright Act, no part may be reproduced by any process
without written permission.

ISBN 0 7309 3615 5

Editor: Gary Dufour
Photographer: Greg Woodward (except pages 2, 6/7, 54/55)
Designer: Trevor Vincent
Printer: Lamb Print

Front cover illustration:
John de Andrea
Allegory: after Courbet 1988
purchased 1989
see text page 63

Back cover illustration:
Worcester Porcelain
'Giles pattern' chestnut basket c1770
gift of Dr Harold Schenberg, 1996
see text page 45

CONTENTS

INTRODUCTION   7

ABORIGINAL ART   10

WESTERN AUSTRALIAN COLONIAL ART   22

HISTORICAL ART   30

CRAFT AND DESIGN   42

CONTEMPORARY ART   52

This book is dedicated to Ella Fry CBE (1916–1997), artist, musician and member of the Board of the Art Gallery of Western Australia from 1956, and its Chairman from 1976 to 1986. Passionately committed to the arts, the Gallery and its future, Ella Fry was instrumental in the continuous improvement of buildings, programs and scholarship devoted to the State Art Collection.

Introduction

The Art Gallery of Western Australia is now over one hundred years old. The Museum and Art Gallery of Western Australia was opened in 1895 by Sir Alexander Onslow, Administrator of the colony. The development reflects an early interest in the future of the arts in Western Australia.

Bernard Woodward, a geologist by profession, was appointed the first curator of the museum, but his interest in and enthusiasm for art led to the first acquisitions for what came to be known as the State Art Collection. These included *Down on his luck* by Frederick McCubbin and *Lake Lugano* by Richard Parkes Bonington. By 1897 the institution was being guided by the advice of such art experts as George Clausen, Edward Poynter, Joshua Lake, James D. Linton, Joseph Pennell and James Reeves. Among the first works acquired were quality British paintings, copies of European masters and a few Australian works.

Until 1908, the State Art Collection was displayed in the overcrowded Museum building, but on 25 June 1908 a new dedicated Art Gallery was officially opened by the Governor of Western Australia, Sir Frederick Bedford. The 'collection' at the time included a display of seventy oils on canvas. The *West Australian* newspaper commented that 'the establishment of the Art Gallery is in keeping with the modern tendency to regard the greatest works of the human genius as the right of the many rather than the perquisite of the few'.

In 1906 George Pitt Morison was appointed Assistant in Art and Craft. After Woodward's retirement as Director in 1916, Pitt Morison remained the only art specialist on staff until his own retirement in 1942. In 1911 an Act of Parliament amalgamated the Library, Museum and Art Gallery into one institution to be administered by a single Board of Trustees. From this time, the interests of the Gallery were subordinated to the needs of the Library and Museum. From 1911, the Gallery existed with a very modest grant from government, and this lack of support continued beyond the end of World War II. However, during the interwar period some significant gifts were made to the Gallery, including Hans Heysen's painting *Droving into the light* and E. Phillips Fox's *Chateau Gaillard*.

In 1926 there was an increase in government funding, specifically for the purchase of books, but in the same year the Gallery received its first significant bequest, of £3000, from Sir John Winthrop Hackett. This proved to be nearly twice as much money as the Government spent on works of art in the forty years from 1911 to 1951. The Hackett Bequest allowed for the acquisition of a number of art works, which included the 1928 purchase of Arthur Streeton's *Barron Gorge* and John Longstaff's *Breaking the news*, acquired in 1933.

World War II brought further financial hardship to the Art Gallery. It had been without a Director since 1916 and it was not until the appointment of Robert Campbell as Director in 1947 that the Gallery's interests were looked after. He was replaced by James Cook in 1950. Both men gave the Gallery a livelier involvement, setting up exhibitions and acquiring works. Cook's connections with the art world outside Western Australia widened the scope and range of the Collection, and during his tenure an Art Gallery Society was formed to bring interested people to the Gallery and to provide a focus for activities such as lectures and demonstrations of artistic methods.

In 1952 Laurie Thomas was appointed Director. His influence was remarkable considering that his term of office encompassed only five years. It was Thomas who provided the true foundation of the present contemporary art holdings, convincing the often reluctant trustees to buy works by contemporary artists and securing an increase in the government grant. Thomas's rapport with artists and his encouragement for young and emerging practitioners created a valuable link between them and the Gallery. However he resigned after a disagreement with the trustees in December 1956. This left a vacuum, as he was not replaced until 1958, when Frank Norton took the helm. Under Norton's guidance over the following eighteen years the Collection grew steadily. During this period a number of sculptures by European artists were acquired: works by Auguste Rodin, Jacob Epstein, Henry Moore and Henri Laurens. It was also at this time that works by Aboriginal artists from Arnhemland and the north of the State were first collected. Meanwhile, in 1955, the Library was separated from the other two institutions, and in 1960 the Art Gallery was separated from the Museum by virtue of an Act of Parliament. With its own Board, the Gallery could concentrate on its own concerns.

Frank Norton's work on the Collection and the growing list of acquisitions only served to make it clear that the building was inadequate and exhibition space very limited. The beginnings of a new era came in 1976, when the Gallery was presented with a fine old building on James Street to house its administrative staff. This building, which is still used for administration, is adjacent to the site where a new building was to be erected. A contract for its construction was signed in 1977. The new Art Gallery building, designed by Perth architect Charles Sierakowski, was built under the guidance of Bertram Whittle, who was appointed Acting Director after Norton's retirement due to ill-health. Frank Ellis, who became Director in 1978, supervised the move into the new building, which was opened on 2 October 1979 by Premier Sir Charles Court. The provision of the building was the principal part of the State Government's contribution to the people in celebration of the 150th anniversary of the founding of Western Australia.

Another important achievement in the 1970s was the re-formation of the Art Gallery Society (later called the Friends of the Art Gallery), which had ceased to exist over the preceding several years. The Society became actively involved in securing acquisitions for the Collection. The members contributed substantially to the purchase of Auguste Rodin's *Adam* and donated works such as *Chorale* by Roger Kemp, *La Zingara* by Arturo Martini, *Outcamp* by Robert Juniper and *Autumn sun, Hunter River Valley* by Lloyd Rees.

Concurrent with the opening of the building, the Gallery launched the Great Australian Paintings Appeal, to bring the standard of the Australian collection into line with the scale and quality of the new building. Support by individuals and businesses made the appeal a great success. As well, substantial assistance was given by the State Government and the Art Gallery Society. With money raised, the Gallery acquired *Moyes Bay, Beaumaris* by Frederick McCubbin and *Dewey eve* by Tom Roberts, among other works.

In 1982 the old Police Court building on Beaufort Street was transferred to the Art Gallery. This grand turn-of-the-century building was refurbished in the mid-1990s under the guidance of Director Paula Latos-Valier and opened by the Premier, the Hon. Richard Court, in July 1995 to mark the Art Gallery's centenary year. In 1997 the Art Gallery, Museum and Library were again combined to form a Ministry for Culture & the Arts.

The Gallery aims to develop the pre-eminent art collection in Western Australia, acquiring, preserving, displaying and promoting the visual arts from the past and present with an emphasis on the heritage of Western Australian art and Aboriginal art and the influences of both Australian and international arts which have informed developments locally.

The State Art Collection now comprises 15,000 works of art. The holdings of Aboriginal art are one of the Gallery's highlights, providing a comprehensive overview of traditional and contemporary works from Arnhemland, the Central Desert and Western Australia. Twentieth-century European and American painting and sculpture are a particular strength, the collection including important works by Stanley Spencer, Frank Auerbach, Ben Nicholson, Medardo Rosso, Aristide Maillol, Lucian Freud, Jean Arp, Mark Tansey and Leon Golub. There is also an extensive holding of prints, drawings and decorative arts, with major movements and styles from the nineteenth and twentieth centuries extensively represented.

In addition to displays from the State Art Collection, the Gallery offers major exhibitions from Australia and overseas as well as special projects and events. Works on view in a permanent display of Western Australian art are rotated continually, and the rest of the Gallery is used to display the Collection in many contexts. Major exhibitions often provide an important platform of reference to the Art Gallery's own holdings. As well, there are public programs for people of all ages, a well-trained group of Voluntary Gallery Guides and a Gallery Art School, as well as a number of special celebrity events throughout the year. Most recently the Art Gallery of Western Australia has taken an active role with the annual Festival of Perth by presenting thought-provoking and appealing exhibitions.

The Friends of the Art Gallery is a public membership organisation dedicated to fund-raising, supporting acquisitions and developing an appreciation of art for its members and the general public. The Art Gallery of Western Australia Foundation was established in 1989 when director, Betty Churcher AO renewed a contemporary focus for the collection and Gallery programs. It is dedicated to raising funds for the future well-being of the Gallery and to enhance its profile within the corporate and private sectors. Several of the Art Gallery's major donors have a gallery named in their honour.

The Art Gallery of Western Australia will continue to be one of the great art galleries of Australia, and it will continue to provide a focus for the development of ideas in the fine arts within the State. As the home of a collection of significant works of art, the Gallery provides an important primary experience with the work itself, giving the viewer a sense of surface, scale and presence not available in any secondary form. As mankind looks more to synthetic experience, for example through computerised data and virtual reality, the increasingly rare confrontation with the artifact of visual ideas will become more and more important. This is why our galleries and art museums must be nurtured, developed and continued.

Alan R. Dodge *Director*

Aboriginal Art

Over the last thirty years Aboriginal art and the status of Aboriginal artists have experienced a dramatic repositioning. Formerly isolated and ignored by critics and galleries, Aboriginal art and artists are now firmly located at the centre of the contemporary Australian art scene. It has been during this important period of change that the holdings of Aboriginal art within the State Art Collection have been developed. This recognition of Aboriginal art and the growing understanding of its wider cultural significance has not, however, been achieved without vigorous agitation for social and political change. The change has in no small measure been influenced by Aboriginal artists themselves often taking a determined and leading role in the process.

In its diversity, Aboriginal art expresses both the distinctiveness of the individual voice and the many regional traditions from across the Australian continent. At the same time there exists a fundamental communality, expressed through an emphasis on the connection between the land and its people and the deep spiritual bond at the core of this relationship.

The art of Arnhemland, with its unbroken connections to ancient ceremonies and materials, presents one such thread of continuity. Its figurative traditions stretch back in an unbroken line to images many thousands of years old, painted onto the faces of rock outcrops and caves. In recent years, successive generations have refined and handed down these traditions.

The relationship between cultural continuity and change is central to the understanding of the paintings of the Papunya artists, whose earliest works, produced in 1971–72, challenged anthropological interpretations of Aboriginal art. These small paintings, with their vivid dotting, enigmatic traditional symbols and narratives linking landscape and mythology, were fundamental in launching a shift in the public perception of the work of Aboriginal artists.

The paintings expressed a strong but at the time little-known art tradition that had existed in ceremonial form for thousands of years in the isolated region of the Central Desert. In the 1980s, when canvases became larger and numbers of new community artists' cooperatives started producing their own variations, individual artists such as Emily Kame Kngwarreye and Abie Jangala achieved wide admiration for their highly original treatment of colour and composition.

The small painted boards of Paddy Tjamitji and the canvases of Rover Thomas reflected a similar desire on the part of Kimberley Aboriginal artists to extend aesthetic boundaries. But these artists remained centrally concerned to maintain the essence of spirituality and cultural identity inherent in their relationship with landscapes of their country. Jimmy Pike also captured the multi-layered flavours of the region with dramatic and complex colour compositions in his re-exploration of the isolated regions of the Great Sandy Desert.

In the light of the 1960s Aboriginal Land Rights Movement and the universal political enfranchisement of all Aboriginal people finally achieved in 1967, a separate generation of artists from urban centres and country areas emerged to add a further dimension to Aboriginal art. Adelaide artist Trevor Nickolls stands as a central figure of this generation, not only in his rejection of the fashions of the day taught to him at art school, but in his tenacious search for an expression that combined engagement with deeply rooted social issues and a contemporary aesthetic idiom.

By the 1980s many other Aboriginal artists, mostly educated in tertiary art schools, had contributed to many themes, stylistic concerns and critical theories of contemporary art in Australia. Among these are Lin Onus, Sally Morgan, Judy Watson, Fiona Foley, Gordon Bennett and Julie Dowling. From their individual personal journeys, these artists share, with a growing viewing public, issues central to Australian society and culture. Today, in its totality, Aboriginal art projects an exuberant and confident character, vital to the present face of Australian art and culture. It also maintains its living links with a heritage of great spiritual strength and complexity.

Michael O'Ferrall

Illustration on previous page:

ANATJARI No. 3 TJAKAMARRA
born c1930 Kurlkurta,
Western Australia
lived and worked at Papunya, Central Desert,
Northern Territory
died 1992
language group: Ngaatjatjarra/Pintupi

Kangaroo rat Dreaming
1972
synthetic polymer on composition board
66 x 57 cm
purchased with funds provided by the
BHP Community Trust to the Art Gallery of
Western Australia Foundation, 1996
(Copyright Aboriginal Artists Agency Ltd,
1997)

The sparseness of this painting is indicative of the essential linear symbolism that lies at the heart of much of the Central Desert aesthetic. The use of only three colours (black, white and red) gives the composition a starkness which appears as a dominant characteristic of Anatjari Tjakamarra's work. The construction of the composition around a series of concentric squares introduces the illusion of three-dimensionality, which led some early commentators to draw comparisons with aspects of 1960s Op Art.

While maintaining a strong adherence to his traditional artistic roots, Anatjari developed a compositional complexity which finds a strong resonance with much contemporary art throughout the world. This feature of his work remains one of many mysteries of a style of art that has developed over thousands of years.

JIMMY PIKE
born 1940 Great Sandy Desert,
Western Australia
lives and works in Broome, Western Australia
language group: Walmajarri

Sandhills in the Simpson Desert
1984
gouache on composition board
123 x 123 cm
purchased 1994

Kimberley artist Jimmy Pike began his career in the early 1980s. Since then his consistent production of prints and paintings has earned him widespread acknowledgment as one of Western Australia's leading artists. He is recognised for his unerring manipulation of colour and strong linear compositions. This work, from early in his career, reveals the bold and skilful manipulation of colour banding, inspired by the rolling sand dunes of the Australian desert landscape. Pike's inspirational imagery stems from the vast range of landscape detail absorbed from his early days growing up in the Great Sandy Desert.

The spiritual beliefs and ritual practices of his tribal background provided another strand of inspiration for his work. Pike's deft counter-positioning of hues from the full range of the colour spectrum creates a bold and assertive statement, suggesting the subtleties and diverse tonal qualities of the central Australian desert.

ROBIN NGANJMIRA
born 1951 western Arnhemland,
Northern Territory
lived and worked in eastern Arnhemland
died 1991
language group: Gunwingku

Dreaming Crocodile – Namanjwarre
1987
ochres on stringy bark
192 x 96 cm
purchased 1991

The untimely death of Robin Nganjmira cut short a promising career as one of the leading figures among a newer generation of western Arnhemland artists. Nganjmira's delicate brushlines captured the lively character of his animal subjects, and his sinuous compositions were full of the life of the bush. The crocodile is the largest and most dangerous of the indigenous animals of the region. As such, it is featured in many important Dreamings of the Kunwinjku people, whose traditional lands are intersected by several major rivers and smaller tributaries where crocodiles are frequently found.

Nganjmira's works are often filled with the teeming life of these waterways as well as pythons and twisting creepers. All these possess natural sinuous forms which the artist takes as his inspiration to build his visually busy compositions. His use of black ochred leaves as a contrast to the white areas of cross-hatching is another device used to enrich the surface of the bark.

ABORIGINAL ART   [13]

FREDDY WEST TJAKAMARRA
born Central Desert, Northern Territory
language group: Pintupi

Snake Dreaming
c1973
gouache, powder paint and synthetic polymer on composition board
46 x 92 cm
purchased 1990
(Copyright Aboriginal Artists Agency Limited, 1997)

Most of the paintings produced in the earliest phase of the Papunya artists' pioneering development possess a delicate miniaturised quality that was largely lost as the scale of paintings grew and the role of coloured dotting became more dominant. These two paintings epitomise the almost fastidious attention to brushstrokes and deft positioning of symbols typical of the Papunya artists during their earliest explorations.

Significant experimentation was needed in the transposition to new artistic formats from body painting and decoration, ground designs, incised and painted symbols on stone and wooden sacred objects, and occasional paintings on rock faces, which formed the core of Aboriginal desert art traditions. One result of this was the incorporation of as many symbolic references as possible in an effort to clarify narrative and spatial dimensions for an outside audience totally unfamiliar with either traditional symbolism or aesthetic conventions. Later concerns about the revelation of information, traditionally only divulged during restricted ceremonies, necessitated substantial compositional and stylistic changes.

[14] ART GALLERY OF WESTERN AUSTRALIA

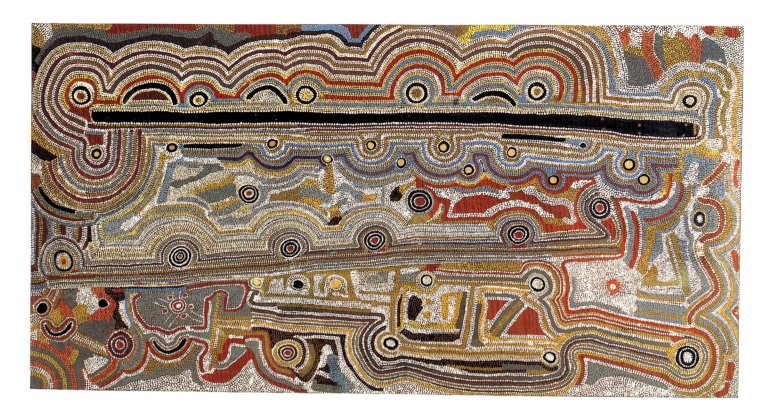

KUMANJAY TJAPALTJARRI SIMS
born 1925, Mt Nicker, Central Desert, Northern Territory
lives and works at Yuendumu, Northern Territory
language group: Warlpiri

Yuwarri Jukurrpa – Milky Way Dreaming
1986
synthetic polymer on canvas
119 x 236 cm
purchased 1992

Yuendumu became the first community to follow in the footsteps of Papunya in establishing an artists' cooperative in the mid-1980s. From the outset the paintings from Yuendumu showed distinct differences. Firstly, the work produced by women artists revealed a substantial area of distinctive and separate gender-based ceremonial and cultural practices hitherto unreported by anthropologists. Secondly, Yuendumu artists were quick to exploit the potential of a full colour range, in contrast to the more restricted red, yellow, black and white palette adopted by most Papunya painters.

Thirdly, as seen in this painting, significant spatial and schematic differences distinguish the works of Yuendumu and Papunya artists. The paintings of Kumanjay Tjapaltjarri Sims have always pushed these spatial and colour differences to produce extremely asymmetrical compositions in which visual energy springs from the tensions of irregularity.

ABORIGINAL ART [15]

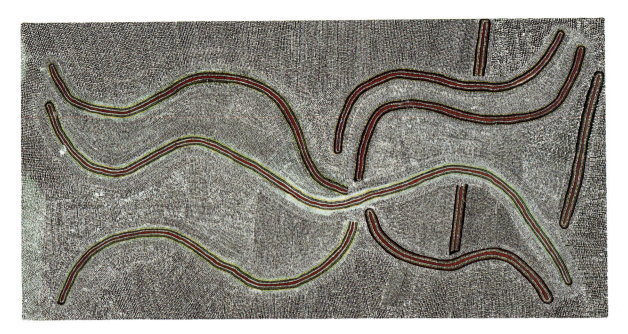

ABIE JANGALA
born c1921 Parnta, Central Desert,
Northern Territory
lives and works at Lagamanu,
Northern Territory
language group: Warlpiri

Ngapa Jukurrpa – Water Dreaming
1989
synthetic polymer on canvas
131 x 264 cm
purchased 1989

Abie Jangala is one of the leading Warlpiri elders in the community of Lajamanu, situated at the northern limits of the Central Desert region. His work is strongly rooted in the great Dreamtime deeds of the Ancestral Beings that once walked the land, creating its features and laying down customs and laws for the Aboriginal inhabitants of this harsh but beautiful part of Australia.

Jangala is among the most distinctive artists to have emerged from the region, and the scale of this painting provides a challenge to the artist's minimalist approach to the use of colour. The long central curving line symbolises a rainstorm (ngapa) as it travels over the landscape. Smaller curving lines represent smaller rain squalls. With these lines, Jangala is using the conventional Aboriginal Central Desert symbol, which also relates to the curved meandering body of a snake and the ground marks it leaves.

This shape also suggests the lines of forked lightning as they flash across the sky. The ultimate visual power of this painting lies, however, in the subtle changes in the white dotted sections artfully counterpoised by the artist. These give the total surface an irregular, rhythmic movement.

EMILY KAME KNGWARREYE
born 1910 Alahalkere (Utopia Station),
Central Desert, Northern Territory
lived and worked in the Central Desert
died 1996
language group: Eastern Anmatyerre

Drying wild flowers in summertime
1991
synthetic polymer on canvas
210 x 120 cm
purchased 1991
(copyright Public Trustee for the
Northern Territory, 1997)

While bearing many of the hallmark symbols of the now well-known Central Desert Aboriginal art movement, Emily Kame Kngwarreye's paintings have always carried a highly distinctive style. This painting is from the period when her canvases first revealed a significant divergence from the central tenets of 'dot and circle' composition. As its title suggests, the artist is responding to the purely surface features of her desert landscape, a landscape that springs into a thousand-colour carpet of flowers and plants whenever the unpredictable rain falls.

Kngwarreye's overlapping splodges of painted dots raise immediate comparisons with techniques employed by the Impressionist movement, with her primary emphasis on the exploration of colour and texture and a clear pleasure in placing paint on canvas. For all these enigmatic comparisons, the originality of Emily Kame Kngwarreye's works commands an immediate response from viewers.

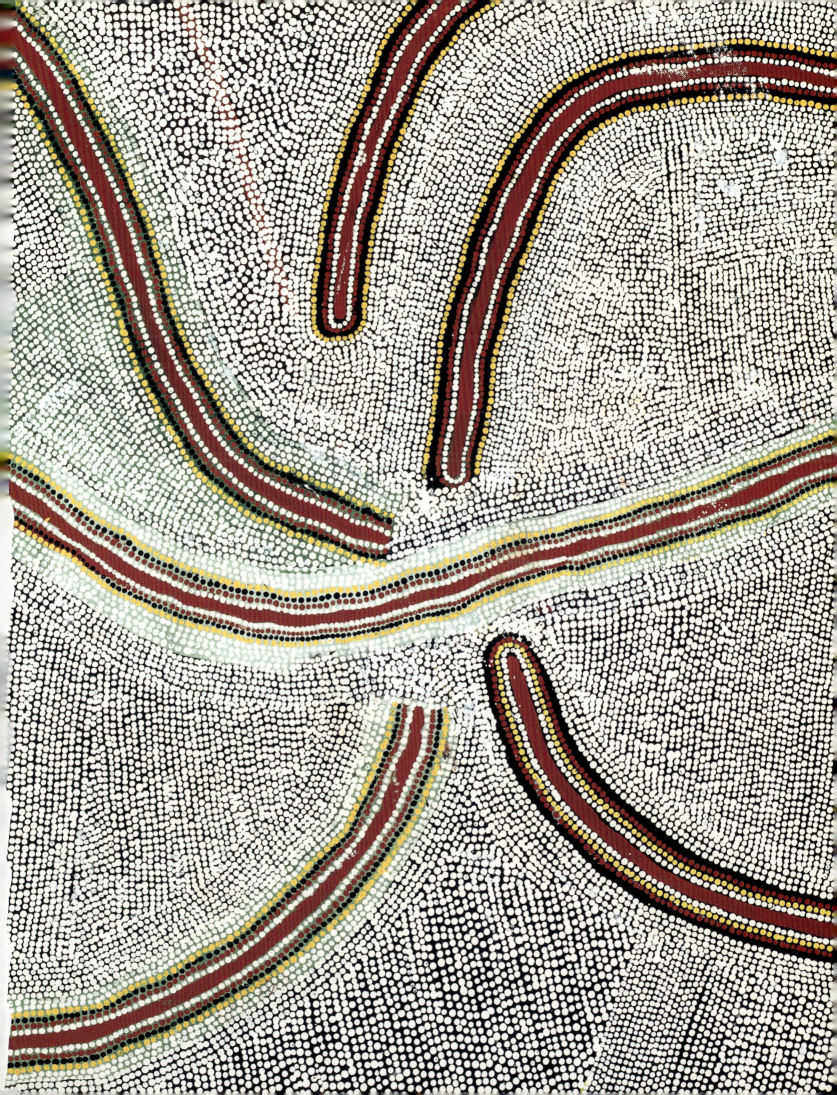

JUDY WATSON
born 1959 Mundubbera, Queensland
lives and works in Sydney
language group: Waanyi

Bloodline
1988
two-colour lithograph with collage
45 x 76 cm
purchased 1989
(© Copyright 1988 Judy Watson.
Reproduced by permission of VI$COPY Ltd,
1997)

As suggested by the title, this work is an evocative reference to the artist's past, her mother's Waanyi tribal country in north-west Queensland and her strong sense of the feminine. Watson's works project an enduring meditational dimension and a serenity of colour and surface treatment that belie her powerful subject matter. The shadowy figures merging with their background suggest ancient cave paintings, evoking the memory of this oldest of Aboriginal forms of art and its highly ritualistic significance.

Watson's career highlights have included winning the prestigious Moët & Chandon Award for 1996 and officially representing Australia at the 1997 Venice Biennale international art exhibition. She has also participated in many residencies and exhibitions in Asia and Europe. Within the contemporary dialogue of intersecting issues and theories, Judy Watson's work is seen as a significant contribution to the discussions of feminism and marginalisation. Her exhibitions in India have found a ready cross-cultural response to her subject of spirituality and the land, which she continues to address in her current work.

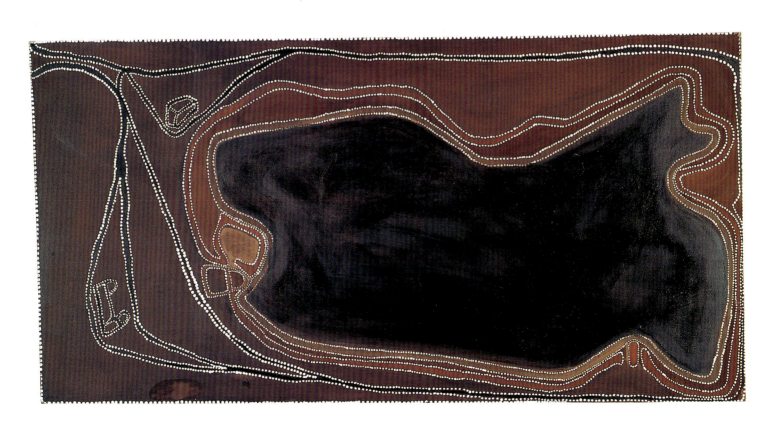

ROVER THOMAS
born c1926 Well 33, Canning Stock Route,
Great Sandy Desert, Western Australia
lives and works at Warmun (Turkey Creek),
East Kimberley, Western Australia
language group: Kukatja/Wangkajunga

Wangkul Junction − Wulangkuya
1988
ochres and gum on canvas
90 x 180 cm
purchased 1988

National recognition of this leading Kimberley artist came in 1990, when his works and those of Trevor Nickolls were chosen to represent Australia at the Venice Biennale exhibition. From the time that his paintings first emerged in the mid-1980s, their raw ochre surfaces and minimal linear composition attracted widespread interest and a unanimous critical response. His experiences in creating the 1975 Gurirr Gurirr ceremony, which combined songs, dances and small dancing boards painted by his uncle Paddy Tjamitji, formed a significant stage in his early development as an artist.

While his paintings produced in the next decade show an undeniable influence from Tjamitji, Rover Thomas's work, in both scale and treatment, is instantly recognisable. Whether the composition is of a secular landscape feature, such as in the painting Wangkul Junction − Wulangkuya, which depicts an aerial view of the Turkey Creek township, or of a particular sacred site in the surrounding countryside, Thomas injects into his canvases a powerful energy that prompts instant comparison with the resonating 'emptiness' of the work of American abstract expressionist Mark Rothko. Thomas's profound encounter with the Kimberley landscape as a stockman remains, part of the fascinating tale of the unconventional pathways followed by Aboriginal artists in their search to maintain and communicate a contemporary spiritual reading of their country's landscape.

TREVOR NICKOLLS
born 1949 Adelaide
lives and works in Adelaide

Political−Spiritual
1981
synthetic polymer on canvas
182 x 60 cm
purchased 1990

This painting comes from an important period in Trevor Nickolls's search for a style and subject matter appropriate to his position as an Aboriginal and an artist working within the wider framework of Australian contemporary art. As had been the case with Albert Namatjira, who forged new artistic pathways in the 1930s and 1940s, Nickolls challenged stereotypical boundaries after graduating from the Art School of South Australia in 1972. Caught in the common 1970s critical view of Aboriginal art as 'separate' and 'primitive', and simultaneously trained during the 'Hard Edge/Colour Field' era, Nickolls has always chosen to follow a highly idiosyncratic and individualistic pathway.

Within his self devised 'Machinetime− Dreamtime' paradigm, the painting Political−Spiritual carries in its message the full weight of his own personal history as well as the baggage of social opinion experienced during his life. The painting carries multiple stylistic references to Cubism and to the art of both Arnhemland and the Central Desert as well as to archetypal symbols from nature. The power of the composition rests on Nickolls's strategic manipulation of these different elements into a single focus, balancing the question of identity and self-portraiture with fundamental notions of nature and culture.

GORDON BENNETT
born 1955 Monto, Queensland
lives and works in Brisbane

The persistence of language
1987
*synthetic polymer on canvas
(triptych), 152 x 411 cm
purchased 1989*

Created during his second year at art school in Brisbane, this painting incorporates many of the key elements that Gordon Bennett has since gone on to refine as part of his broad-ranging subject matter. During his career Bennett has produced numerous compositions that position him as a leading contributor to the development of Australian art since the late 1980s. His paintings and writings have also figured prominently within international post-colonialism debates. Intellectually, his work has not only impacted on fundamental Australian political and social questions, but contributed to the understanding of the dramatic impact of the new interactive global order, alternative readings of identity and a necessary revision of an exclusively European view of colonial history.

The monochromatic treatment in this painting provides a basis for the subject matter, which deals with both the Australian era of black deaths in custody and the artist's own experiences and responses to the extremities of racism. With its unequivocal emotional message the work reveals a visual rawness. However it communicates a mature emotional 'edge' which Bennett has maintained.

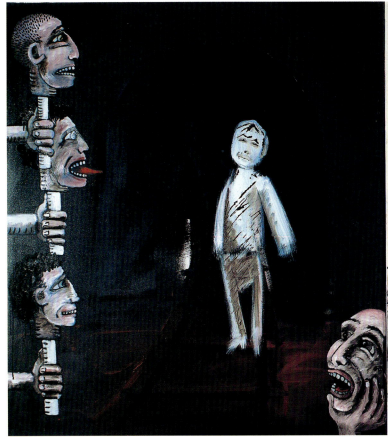

LIN ONUS
born 1948 Melbourne
lived and worked in Upwey, Victoria
died 1996
Language group: Yorta Yorta

Maralinga
1990
fibreglass, pigment, plexiglass, paper stickers
figure: 163 cm high;
cloud: 125 x 119 x 45 cm
purchased 1990

While Melbourne artist Lin Onus is known primarily for his paintings, equally fundamental are his three-dimensional works. Onus developed an incisive eye for the issues and arguments relating to Aboriginal Land Rights, using the landscapes of both Victoria and Arnhemland as paradigms for displacement and the emotional dislocation experienced by Aboriginal people.

The inspiration for Maralinga grew directly out of his exposure to the central Australian landscape and visual experiences gained during his frequent road trips between Melbourne and Arnhemland. As the Australian desert site for atomic bomb tests conducted by England in the early 1950s, Maralinga has become an enduring symbol for both the desecration and the pollution of the landscape. It is also a potent commentary on the compulsory displacement of its Aboriginal landholders from their traditional land. In the realistic treatment of the mother and child sheltering each other from the bomb's lethal wind blast, the composition carries an additional message as a potent evocation of the human desolation caused by all wars and instruments of war. The perspex mushroom cloud and radioactivity symbols act as a pointer to the specific events at Maralinga.

Lin Onus has been awarded an Order of Australia for his services to the arts as painter, sculptor and promotor of Aboriginal artists and their works.

ABORIGINAL ART

Western Australian Colonial Art

The country's most comprehensive collection of early pictorial material relating to the western third of Australia is held by the Art Gallery of Western Australia. Comprising nearly four hundred oil paintings, prints and drawings and watercolours, this section of the State Art Collection covers the social and material progress of Western Australia from pre-settlement times through to the granting of responsible government in 1890. Works of art, colonial furniture and heritage objects are acquired to illustrate different aspects of the region and its material and social development as a British colony, as well as the evolving story of the visual arts.

The western coast has Australia's longest recorded history of European contact. Before the British established a permanent settlement at Albany on the south coast of Western Australia in 1826, the region was frequently visited by Dutch, French and British expeditions mapping the coastline and gathering scientific information. The Dutch were familiar with the area well before the east coast was first visited by European explorers. The earliest documented contact was in 1616, when the Dutch captain Dirck Hartog charted offshore islands in the North-West. The earliest visual images date from William de Vlamingh's visit in 1697, when he landed at Rottnest Island and the shores of the Swan River. Regular accounts by French and British topographic and scientific artists after 1800 provide detailed information about the environment and the complex and fluctuating relationships between Europeans and Aborigines.

The State Art Collection contains significant images of encounters between Aboriginals and Europeans. Aspects of traditional Aboriginal life and culture are illustrated in a range of works that pre-date British colonisation. Drawings by Phillip Parker King of his meeting with Aboriginal people in the Albany area in 1821 are complemented by a series of lithographs made by French artist Louis De Sainson after he visited the region only months before the British established the first permanent settlement in Albany in 1826. A folio of twenty-two watercolours and drawings by Richard Ffarington illustrates Aboriginal life and customs in the south-west of the State in the 1840s and watercolours by convict artist James Walsh record the displacement of Aborigines around Perth as the town expanded in the 1860s.

The history of the visual arts in Western Australia has been dominated by an engagement with landscape. Artists trained in topographic or scientific drafting frequently accompanied voyages of discovery as imperial powers competed to find potential territories for colonisation. They were important and influential agents in constructing images of a new land for dissemination to a European audience. The early nineteenth-century images illustrate the imposition of conventional formulas of a European picturesque tradition onto an unfamiliar landscape, and by the close of the century artists influenced by Impressionism were beginning to establish careers in Western Australia. The discovery of gold deposits in the Coolgardie–Kalgoorlie area and the Kimberley in the 1880s led to the rapid expansion of the colony and an influx of gold-seekers from around the world. Many professionally trained artists were attracted to Western Australia by new opportunities.

Janda Gooding *Curator Historical Art*

FREDERICK GARLING
born 1806 London, England
arrived Australia 1815
active in Western Australia 1827
died Sydney, 1873

View across the coastal plain
1827
watercolour
13 x 37 cm
purchased 1978

In early 1827 Captain James Stirling was commissioned by the British Government to investigate the Swan River area and comment on its prospects for settlement. The exploration party arrived in March 1827 and travelled up the Swan River. They camped near Guildford, and Stirling's journal entry for 15 March noted the view from nearby hills: 'As far as the eye could carry, Northward, Southward, and Westward, lay extended an immense plain covered in general with Forest and varied by occasional eminences and glimpses of the River winding through it.' Accompanying him on the journey was a young naval officer, Frederick Garling, who recorded their journey with a series of delicate watercolours. Garling's visual records and Stirling's persuasive official report to the British authorities combined to praise the region for its natural harbours, wooded plains, fertile soil and abundant fresh water. Two years later Stirling returned as the first Lieutenant Governor of the new Swan River Colony. The towns of Perth and Fremantle were founded and the colony later renamed Western Australia.

after ROBERT DALE
born 1810 Winchester, Hampshire, England
active in Albany, Western Australia 1829
died Bath, England, 1833
ROBERT HAVELL, engraver

Panoramic view of King George's Sound, part of the colony of Swan River (detail)
1834
hand-coloured etching and aquatint
18 x 274 cm
purchased 1955

The panorama was a popular art form in the early nineteenth century. Viewers could see a complete 360-degree view of extensive landscapes at specially constructed round halls. This panorama of Albany was published in London in 1834, only eight years after the settlement had been founded. Albany was a remote outpost of the British Empire, originally intended as a penal colony. The scene was sketched by Lieutenant Robert Dale, stationed there from January to May 1832. From the elevated position of Mt Clarence, above the township, Dale has accurately recorded the topographical features, while in the foreground human dramas are enacted. The original inhabitants, the Meananger people, are shown possuming and returning from a fishing expedition. On the right a group of soldiers comes back from a kangaroo hunt and is met by an Aborigine dressed in European clothes. This is probably Nakinna, the leader of the group. Dale's panorama presents an interesting and reassuring view of the region for a London audience, but fails to illustrate the constant tension and friction between the two groups.

[24]   ART GALLERY OF WESTERN AUSTRALIA

THOMAS TURNER
born 1813 London, England
active in Western Australia 1830–1852
died Melbourne, 1895

Albion House Augusta
1836
pen and ink and watercolour
14 x 33 cm
gift of Mr J. R. Turner, 1929

The Turner family emigrated to the new Swan River Colony in early 1830. They brought considerable capital and at least seven labourers, some of whom were accompanied by their families. On arrival in Western Australia, they found that all the best agricultural land around the Swan River was already allocated. Together with other settlers, they established a new settlement at Augusta, 320 kilometres to the south of Perth. Thomas Turner's view of their new property shows the order that Europeans imposed on the Australian landscape. The English-style house sits overlooking cultivated land neatly protected by fences. On all sides, the partly cleared bush acts as a buffer between the known and the unknown. Albion House was originally erected on Seine Bay, Augusta, where it was the home of the Turner family. It is believed that the bricks were imported from England. It was dismantled in 1849 and re-erected in Adelaide Terrace, Perth, where it was known as Lismore House. It was eventually demolished in 1946.

GEORGE NASH
active in Western Australia 1838–1848

An extensive view of Perth, Western Australia, with a group of natives in the foreground
c1846
watercolour and pencil highlighted with bodycolour
36 x 54 cm
purchased through the Geoffrey William Robinson Bequest, 1992

Mount Eliza overlooks the capital city of Perth and is a natural vantage point for viewing the Swan River, the flood plains and the distant Darling Ranges. From as early as 1827, European artists had depicted the scene as one of Arcadian peace, prosperity and progress. This watercolour was painted in about 1846 by George Nash. Nineteenth-century visiting artists like Nash were well acquainted with the picturesque formula of landscape painting still predominant in Britain. Groups of Aborigines were often included in the foreground to assist developing a sense of scale, but this also served to reassure prospective migrants of the ability of military authorities to maintain peace and order in the colony. Despite vigorous and often violent resistance to the taking of their land, by 1846 the Aborigines from around Perth were mainly housed in the Native Institution, which had been established at the base of Mount Eliza.

LOUISA CLIFTON
born 1814 London, England
active in Western Australia from 1841
died Geraldton, Western Australia, 1880

View of the temporary residence of the Chief Commissioner at Australind
c1841–42
watercolour and pencil
20 x 37 cm
purchased through the Geoffrey William Robinson Bequest, 1994

Louisa Clifton arrived in Western Australia with her family in 1841. Her father, Marshall Waller Clifton, was the Chief Commissioner in charge of the new development at Australind, south of Perth. The settlement's name embodied the hope that it would become a centre of trade between Australia and India. The Western Australian Company launched the commercial scheme according to the theories of Edward Gibbon Wakefield, who advocated that land should be sold to settlers and the proceeds used to bring labourers to the colony. Altogether, four hundred immigrants arrived, living in rough tents with rushes on the floor until more permanent dwellings could be built. The settlement failed within a few years due to poor sandy soils, lack of farming experience and insufficient capital. By 1846 the company had been wound up and most settlers had drifted away or left the colony. Delicate watercolours by Louisa and her sister Mary record both the optimism and the disappointments of the Australind scheme.

HENRY PRINSEP
born 1844 Calcutta, India
active in Western Australia from 1866
died Busselton, Western Australia, 1922

Ularring (Attacked) woodhouse feud
c1876
pen and ink and watercolour
12 x 20 cm
purchased 1970

In 1875 Ernest Giles, an explorer, left Port Augusta in South Australia to cross to the Indian Ocean in the west. A confrontation occurred between the Europeans and a group of Aborigines at a well in the Everard Ranges. Henry Prinsep, an English-trained artist who emigrated to Western Australia in 1866, later illustrated the published account of the journey. He has shown the Europeans preparing to fire, while Aborigines friendly to the party attempt to intervene. The Aboriginal group eventually withdrew. Many of Prinsep's sketches recording explorations within Western Australia are held by the Gallery, including several preparatory drawings for this watercolour. Henry Prinsep was a founding member of the first art societies in Western Australia in the 1890s, and he was enthusiastically involved in amateur musicals, theatre and set design. In his career as a civil servant, he later became Head of the Aborigines Department.

RICHARD ATHERTON FFARINGTON
born 1823 England
active in Western Australia 1843–47
died Lancashire, England, 1855

Corroboree or native dance
c1843–47
watercolour and pencil
27 x 17 cm
purchased 1984

In 1984 the Art Gallery purchased an important folio of drawings and watercolours depicting the life and customs of Aboriginal people of the south-west of Western Australia. The artist was Richard Atherton Ffarington, who created his images between 1843 and 1847. His sensitive portrayals and accurate descriptions of daily activities provide visual confirmation of details otherwise only accessible through written and oral accounts. Ffarington provides us with a spectator's view of a night scene in which a line of male dancers emerges from the shadows. The lead dancer is painted with white horizontal stripes and a line running down his back. It was common for Europeans to observe such scenes, but Corroboree or native dance is a rare depiction of Aboriginal ritual life in early nineteenth century Western Australia. Very few images of ceremonial dance are known.

Historical Art

Public collections are organic structures, constantly shifting and refining emphasis according to the times and people involved. Including paintings, sculpture and works on paper, historical art in the State Art Collection has been accumulated over the last hundred years. It is a comparatively young Collection, and its history is marked by periods of great inactivity interspersed with years of inspired and aggressive purchasing. With the Collection having been shaped by relatively few curators, some idiosyncratic developments are apparent, giving it a character unique among the Australian State collections.

From its foundation in 1895, the State Art Gallery drew upon British expertise and buyers. Their advice resulted in the establishment of a strong foundation for the Collection during its first fifteen years. An emphasis was placed on obtaining representative examples of the British School, paintings by Thomas Gainsborough, Thomas Lawrence, Richard Parkes Bonington, Richard Wilson, Wilson Steer and George Clausen being acquired, together with works on paper by Aubrey Beardsley, Anning Bell, Walter Crane and Charles Keene. In more recent times, the collection of British art has been substantially built upon with the acquisition of works by artists of the Bloomsbury and Camden Town schools and early abstracts by Ben Nicholson, Barbara Hepworth, Peter Lanyon, Victor Passmore and William Scott. The Gallery's most significant British art acquisition is Stanley Spencer's *Christ in the wilderness* 1939–43, purchased in 1983.

Figurative art is a strength within the Collection. This finds outstanding expression in a small group of European sculpture that includes work by Auguste Rodin, Emil-Antoine Bourdelle, Jaques Lipchitz, Aristide Maillol, Ernst Barlach, Giacomu Manzu, Arturo Martini, Auguste Renoir, Henri Laurens and Jean Arp. Other aspects of European Modernism are well represented in the print collection, with fine examples by Pablo Picasso, Emil Nolde, Ludwig Kirchner, Max Beckmann, Laszlo Moholy-Nagy and El Lissitzky.

Non-Western material in the State Art Collection is focused primarily on Japanese art. Through prints and craftwork, a continuing dialogue between Japanese and Australian art and design is demonstrated. A selection of woodblock prints, mostly purchased in 1902 from the Imperial Museum in Tokyo, provided a solid foundation for purchases of contemporary Japanese prints from the 1960s.

The State Art Collection has outstanding late nineteenth-century Australian paintings. Frederick McCubbin's *Down on his luck* 1889, one of Australia's iconic Heidelberg school paintings, was acquired in 1896. The addition in 1933 of John Longstaff's *Breaking the news* 1887 gave the collection a strong focus on figurative and narrative work. Although the representation of Australian art did not receive a high priority during the early years of the Gallery's growth, fine colonial paintings by John Glover, Eugene von Guérard, Haughton Forrest and Nicholas Chevalier have formed a core group of nineteenth-century works. Central to the representation of modern Australian art are examples by Margaret Preston, Kathleen O'Connor, Russell Drysdale, Sidney Nolan and Ian Fairweather.

Consistent with its aims to collect, research and display Western Australian art, the State Art Collection has the most comprehensive selection of historical art produced in the State. Detailed representation of the colonial period provides a unique focus, and there are works by all major Western Australian artists. Highlights include fine examples of the work of early women artists, including Florence Fuller and Daisy Rossi, and Western Australian printmakers of the interwar period – Beatrice Darbyshire, Edith Trethowan and A.B. Webb. Recent research in the field of sculpture has seen pieces by Edward Kohler and Hetty Finlay acquired to complement later sculptures by Margaret Priest and Howard Taylor. Photographic activity is represented by substantial holdings of work by Hal Missingham, Axel Poignant and members of the pictorialist Van Raalte club. Many of the State's leading contemporary artists established their careers between the late 1940s and 1960; these included artists such as Elizabeth Durack, Howard Taylor, Guy Grey-Smith, Elise Blumann and Robert Juniper, all of whom are represented.

Janda Gooding *Curator Historical Art*

EUGENE VON GUÉRARD
born 1811 Vienna, Austria
active in Australia 1852–81
died Chelsea, England, 1901

Mt William from Mt Dryden, Victoria
1857
oil on canvas
62 x 91 cm
purchased 1971

Von Guérard introduced a different and very northern European way of looking at the Australian landscape. Trained in the German Romantic tradition, he sought to express the divine power of nature in his paintings. In 1856 he visited the Grampians area in western Victoria and painted this view of Mt William, the highest point in the ranges. The mountain rises majestically in the distance, surrounded by a sublimely glowing sky. Details are meticulously recorded, from the tree-covered plain to the rocks in the foreground. However, a reminder of the violence of nature and of European impact on the environment can also be found in the introduced fox stalking the kangaroos in the foreground.

JOHN GLOVER
born 1767 Houghton-on-the-Hill, Leicester, England
active in Tasmania from 1831
died Tasmania, 1849

Patterdale, Van Dieman's Land
1834
oil on canvas
76 x 117 cm
purchased through the Great Australian Paintings Appeal with funds presented by Westralian Forest Industries, 1978

After a successful career in Britain as a landscape artist, John Glover and his wife emigrated to Tasmania in 1831 to join their sons. In 1832 he took up land and called his farm Patterdale after a property he had owned in the Lakes District of England. In coming to terms with the unfamiliar landscape of Australia, Glover had to reassess his indebtedness to a picturesque style of composition. He looked afresh at the sinuous eucalypt trees, the strong clear light and the straggly, more confused nature of the Australian bush, which often closed off vistas rather than presented an expansive landscape. Patterdale, Van Dieman's Land shows the natural and the human landscapes interacting and in harmony. Glover is often acknowledged as one of the first European artists to faithfully capture the essence of the Australian landscape.

FREDERICK MCCUBBIN
born 1855 Melbourne, Victoria
died Melbourne, 1917

Down on his luck
1889
oil on canvas
114 x 153 cm
purchased 1896

When it was first exhibited in 1889, a reviewer noted Down on his luck *as 'thoroughly Australian in spirit, and yet so poetic that it is a veritable bush idyll...' (*Table Talk *26 April 1889). In the 1890s, the painting symbolised a passing way of life: that of itinerant bush workers 'on the wallaby track'. It evoked nostalgia for a time when it was possible for independent gold prospectors or bushmen to make a simple living and choose to move on when they wished.*

The landscape elements for Down on his luck *were probably painted outdoors at Box Hill, close to Melbourne. However the figure, modelled by McCubbin's friend and fellow artist Louis Abrahams, was completed in the studio. Although strongly tied to the social and political climate of the late nineteenth century,* Down on his luck *has continued to appeal to viewers since its purchase by the Gallery in 1896. Its melancholy portrayal of an individual deep in thought and surrounded by landscape finds sympathetic responses from contemporary audiences.*

Down on his luck is complemented by another great narrative picture, John Longstaff's Breaking the news, 1887. *A dramatic scene of the personal tragedy of a mining disaster, Longstaff's painting fullfilled all the requirements of a sentimental Victorian narrative picture. When it was shown in 1887 it was praised for its 'Australianness', but the event and scene are universal.* Breaking the news *won Longstaff the gold medal awarded to the best art student at the National Gallery of Victoria School in 1887 as well as a travelling scholarship of £150 per year with the opportunity to study in Europe.*

HISTORICAL ART   [33]

STANLEY SPENCER
born 1891 Cookham on Thames,
Berkshire, England
died Clivedon, Avon, England, 1959

**Christ in the wilderness:
Rising from sleep in the morning**
1940
oil on canvas
56 x 56 cm
purchased 1983
(© Copyright 1940 Stanley Spencer.
Reproduced by permission of VI$COPY Ltd,
1997)

When Stanley Spencer started this series in 1939, his personal relationships were disintegrating and he was living in a small flat in London. He empathised with Christ's experience of forty days and nights in the wilderness, and sought a way of incorporating elements of his own life into an interpretation of the biblical story. Spencer's original concept for the Christ in the wilderness *series was forty paintings, representing one for each day. Although he drew up the grid on which to base the series, it was subsequently modified. In the sketches and paintings in the State Art Collection, Spencer has celebrated the unity of Christ with all living things, from the scorpion he holds in his palm to the hens, lilies and foxes. In* Rising from sleep in the morning, *Spencer has illustrated Luke 15:18 – 'I will arise and go to my Father'. The monumental figure shrouded in a simple robe rises from the earth like a flower opening at the start of day. However, the pit is also reminiscent of a bomb crater, reminding us of Spencer's experience in the Ambulance Corps during World War I. In 1981 the Art Gallery of Western Australia purchased the entire collection of nine paintings of Stanley Spencer's* Christ in the wilderness *series together with sixteen preliminary drawings. Along with other works by Spencer, including a fine painting* Christ evicting the money changers, *1921, and a substantial collection of drawings, the Gallery has the finest holdings of this artist's work in Australia.*

WILLIAM BLAKE
born 1757 London, England
died London, 1827

The fall of Satan
plate 16 from *The Book of Job*
1825
engraving
120 x 16 cm
purchased 1970

William Blake's The Book of Job *combines a singular creative vision of the fate of humankind with complete command over the engraving medium. Blake had been interested in the story of Job from as early as 1786, when he made a watercolour of 'Job's complaint'. In 1823, at the request of his friend John Linnell, he commenced a series of engravings based on watercolour illustrations he had made for his patron, Thomas Butts, in 1805. With* The Book of Job, *the text and illustrations were executed simultaneously in one process by Blake. The engravings have additional marginal text and designs to emphasise Blake's belief that Job had erred spiritually. Job's attention to the laws of religion, rather than their spiritual basis, leads him to a fallen state of self-pity and self-righteousness. However, through his faith he is eventually restored. Blake's* The Book of Job *is a powerful and personal response to the Old Testament story, its emotional intensity a tribute to Blake's visionary powers.*

HISTORICAL ART   [35]

IAN FAIRWEATHER
born 1891 Bridge of Allan, England
lived and worked on Bribie Island
died Bribie Island, Queensland 1974

Monsoon
1961–62
synthetic polymer and gouache on cardboard
98 x 188 cm
purchased 1983
(© Copyright 1962 Ian Fairweather.
Reproduced by permission of VI$COPY Ltd,
1997)

In November 1961 a wild storm lashed Bribie Island off the Queensland coast. Fairweather's hut remained intact, but thirteen trees around it were flattened. For the artist it recalled a terrifying experience during his raft voyage from Darwin to Timor in 1952. The sky became like a dense wall as a monsoon descended upon him. He described the approaching storm clouds as 'white towers with flashes of lightning striking from their bases in the sea'. It was these visions that inspired Monsoon, *a large work that is acknowledged as one of Fairweather's finest paintings. He built up the image using layers of paint and gouache in a simple palette of greys and blacks evocative of the night. The jagged white and cream marks become the lightning striking down. Through it all, the artist's respect for calligraphy is evident in the image and the physicality of the paint as it drips towards the lower edges.*

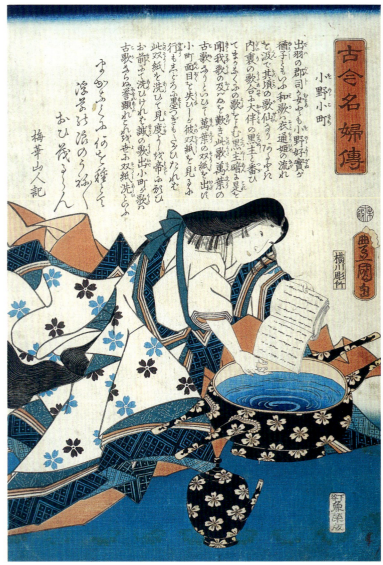

A. B. WEBB
born 1887 Ashford, Kent, England
active in Perth from 1915
died Perth, 1944

The fisherman, misty morning
c1921–22
colour woodcut
16 x 16 cm
purchased 1996

The fisherman, nocturne
c1921–22
colour woodcut
24 x 17 cm
gift of Miss Edith Tothill, 1978

Webb studied in England and worked as a commercial artist before emigrating to Western Australia in 1915. He was a highly skilled watercolourist and draughtsman, whose imagery usually illustrated the quieter and more harmonious landscapes of Western Australia. In about 1921 he started to experiment with printmaking, adopting the traditional Japanese method of hand-colouring the individual blocks and then hand-printing. He achieved sensitive gradations of colour similar to watercolour washes, and his method of work ensured that each print pulled from the edition was subtly different. On occasions Webb would cut down the blocks or vary the colours dramatically to produce different effects, as in these atmospheric scenes of a fisherman on the Swan River at morning and evening. Through his position as Art Master at Perth Technical College and his own A.B. Webb School of Art, he had considerable influence on the development of printmaking and watercolour painting in Western Australia between the wars. His contribution is acknowledged through the comprehensive collection of his work at the Art Gallery.

UTAGAWA KUNISADA
1786–1864 Edo, Japan

The poetess – Onono Komachi
colour woodcut
36 x 25 cm
purchased from the Imperial Museum, Tokyo, 1902

In 1902 the Art Gallery of Western Australia established a small collection of Japanese art with purchases of woodblock prints and objects from the Imperial Museum, Tokyo. Prints by Kunisada, Kuniteru, Kuniyoshi, Sadahide and Toyokuni were selected. The Gallery has built on these early foundations by adding both historical and contemporary prints and objects. Kunisada was one of the masters of the Utagawa School of Ukiyo-e Japanese woodblock printing, which became well known for its illustrations of popular stories, representations of Kabuki theatre actors and colourful scenes of middle-class life. Kunisada's superb technique and stylised pattern-making are evident in this portrait of the famous woman poet Onono Komachi. In the late nineteenth century, Ukiyo-e prints such as this were enthusiastically collected by European artists, who were intrigued by the bold designs and flattened perspective.

ERNST LUDWIG KIRCHNER
born 1880 Aschaffenburg, Germany
lived and worked Dresden and Davos, Switzerland
died Frayenkirch, Germany, 1938

Woman in a hat
1911
oil on canvas

The pledge – Hutten greets Sickingen
1923–24
oil on canvas
95 x 85 cm
gift of Baron H. H. Thyssen-Bornemisza, 1979

To celebrate the opening of the Art Gallery of Western Australia's new building in 1979, Baron Thyssen-Bornemisza presented Woman in a hat *1911 by Ernst Ludwig Kirchner. The model for* Woman in a hat *sits in a strong frontal position. Kirchner has created a series of angular and uncomfortable forms, with the body literally pushing against the frame edge. Inspired by African sculptures, Kirchner sought to unite all elements of the picture into an expressive and passionate whole. On the reverse side of the canvas is* The pledge – Hutten greets Sickingen, *painted in 1923–24 after Kirchner's move to the Swiss mountains, where he sought to recuperate from physical and mental breakdowns. It illustrates his desire to return to earlier artistic influences. Drawing upon his Fauvist compositions, Persian rug designs and Coptic tapestries, he created images that were more decorative and tended toward being two-dimensional.* The pledge *is typical of his 'tapestry style' in its vibrant colour and strong vertical and horizontal composition. It portrays the sixteenth-century humanist Ulrich Hutten meeting Franz von Sickingen, a nationalistic fighter against corruption and foreign dominance.*

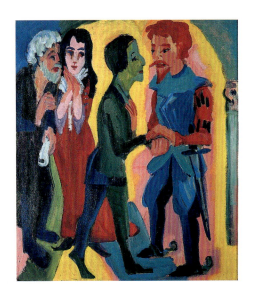

KATHLEEN O'CONNOR
born 1876 Hokitika, New Zealand
active in Perth 1902–06,
active in Paris 1906–39, lived in London 1939–45, active in Paris 1945–49,
active in Perth from 1949
died Perth, 1968

The tea table (L'heure du thé)
c1928
tempera on card
80 x 100 cm
purchased 1949

The tea table is one of Kathleen O'Connor's most accomplished paintings, executed in Paris during the late 1920s when she experimented with the tempera medium. At first glance it is a casual teatime setting for two. But there is nothing casual about the composition, which is complex and carefully manipulated. The bright palette of pinks, orange and acid yellow is balanced with the cool rationality of grey and white. Many of her favourite domestic objects are included in the scene. By tilting the table edge forward and using the brightly coloured patterned oriental carpet as a backdrop, O'Connor has closed off any sense of real space. After nearly fifty years working in Paris, from 1906 to 1955, O'Connor eventually returned to Western Australia. In view of her strong associations with Western Australia, the Art Gallery has acquired a comprehensive collection of her work, including paintings, watercolours, drawings and textile designs.

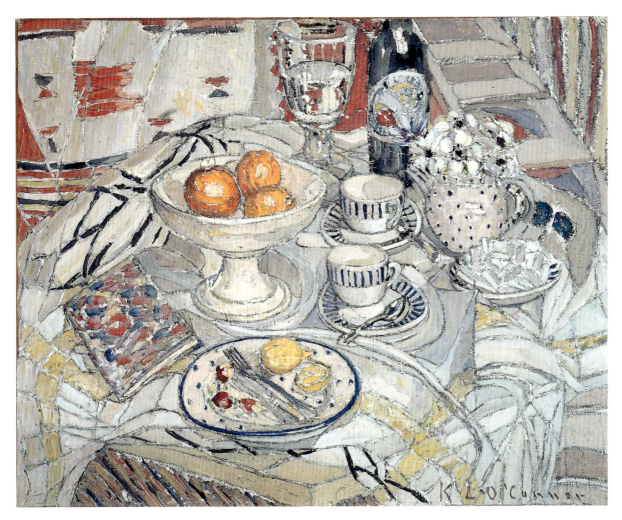

ELISE BLUMANN
born 1897 Parchim, Germany
active in Perth from 1938
died Perth, 1990

Storm on the Swan
1946
oil on paper on composition board
58 x 68 cm
gift of Elizabeth Lefroy, 1984

Elise Blumann, her husband and young son arrived in Western Australia in 1938. Her training in Germany had instilled a desire to express artistically her relationship with the natural environment. In Australia she painted the local landscape along the river at Nedlands, often using a huge melaleuca tree close to her home as a central motif. In this she has reduced the tree to a single gnarled and twisted mass, shaped by the river winds. All detail is eroded away. Blumann was a strong advocate of the importance of art education in the personal development of individuals, and she pursued this in her role as an art teacher.

HISTORICAL ART

BEN NICHOLSON
born 1894 Denham, England
lived and worked in London
active in Switzerland 1958–72
died London, 1982

Still life
1945
oil on hardboard
58 x 54 cm
purchased 1967
(© Copyright 1945 Ben Nicholson. Reproduced by permission of VI$COPY Ltd, 1997)

Ben Nicholson provides a strong link between European and British abstraction. Through his connections to the Abstraction-Création group in Paris and his involvement with the London-based Unit One group, he was in touch with many of the leading practitioners of abstract and Constructivist art of the interwar years. Nicholson first visited Cornwall in 1928 and returned there to live in 1939. Together with a number of other artists, including Barbara Hepworth, Naum Gabo and Peter Lanyon, he was involved in establishing at St Ives a community devoted to abstract art. This work was painted in St Ives towards the end of that period, when he returned to working in the studio on still life subjects. It was a period of reflection and introspection. Nicholson explored the problems of line, form and space in delicate and intricate still life compositions that show his complete control of surface and composition.

[40]   Art Gallery of Western Australia

GUY GREY-SMITH
born 1916 Wagin, Western Australia
active in London 1945–48
died Pemberton, Western Australia, 1981

Skull Springs country
1966
oil and beeswax emulsion on hardboard
122 x 183 cm
purchased 1967

Guy Grey-Smith first became interested in art in 1940 when he was a prisoner of war in Germany. After his release, he spent some time at the Chelsea School of Art in London, where he was exposed to modern developments in art. However, on his return to Western Australia in 1948, he investigated earlier stylistic trends, learning from Cézanne, the Impressionists and the Fauves. Each year from the late 1950s he and his family would travel to the north-west of Western Australia. He found that the strong light and unique geological features of the region suited his purpose of distilling the landscape into structural slabs of colour and mass. In 1969 Grey-Smith said that the lessons of Nicolas de Stael gave him greater freedom in the physical process of painting: 'I think the pleasure of painting is the manipulation of this solid body – that it's pushed around into a kind of structure – the thickness of paint or impasto, not for its own sake but the physical pleasure of having enough stuff to push around.'

HISTORICAL ART [41]

Craft and Design

In his 1901 Annual Report, art collection curator Bernard Woodward wrote: 'The number of specimens of metalwork, pottery, etc., has been considerably increased and by the time the new galleries are completed, this very valuable and instructive service must prove of much benefit to the art workers and artisans of this State.'

The century thus began with contemporary craft and design items being acquired and shown to an eager and appreciative audience. By 1911, however, the Art Gallery's growth was severely reduced when Parliament established an amalgamated State Library, Museum and Art Gallery. While gifts were accepted, it would be sixty-seven years before a curatorial department for Craft and Design was formed and acquisitions made according to a clearly defined policy.

In developing the collection, Woodward sought advice and suggestions from a number of colleagues in Britain, Europe and Japan. Contacts in the English Art Workers' Guild resulted in the early predominance of Arts and Crafts Movement purchases. Locally, advice was sought from the State's pre-eminent studio craftsman, James W.R. Linton. A painter, silversmith and furniture designer/maker, Linton established in Western Australia the style of the British Arts and Crafts Movement, influential since the 1870s for its reliance on simple craft-based design and use of materials. Important works by British craftworkers such as silversmiths Nelson Dawson, Omar Ramsden and Alexander Fisher, along with pieces from the Doulton, Della Robbia, Liberty and Wedgwood companies, began to define this section of the State Art Collection and exert an influence on local artists.

Early acquisitions were in many cases the result of exchanges, with unusual contemporary European work coming into the State Art Collection. The most notable is a group of St Petersburg Imperial Porcelain Factory vases in the Art Nouveau style, a rare sight in any museum, let alone a museum on the rim of the Indian Ocean in 1909!

Purchases of Royal Copenhagen and Meissen porcelain, Austrian Loetz glass, American Rookwood pottery and a group of late Meiji Period Japanese ceramics, lacquer, ivory and metalwork lent an increasingly international character to the holdings. Disappointingly, no Australian craft or design works were acquired in this early period, and even Linton's work would not be purchased until 1986.

The Gallery appointed a Curator of Craft and Design in 1978 in response to the burgeoning Australian crafts revival of the 1970s. The turn-of-the-century acquisitions provided a foundation on which to build a cohesive representation of the development of craft and design from the mid-eighteenth century to the present. There is a good representation of contemporary studio crafts and the industrial and decorative design that form such a rich part of late twentieth century visual culture. Through the ceramics, glass, textiles, jewellery, metalwork and furniture in the holdings, it is possible to trace the complex relationships between craft, design and contemporary culture from the late nineteenth to the end of the twentieth century.

The Art Gallery of Western Australia embraces the field of craft and design within the three major focuses in the State Art Collection: Western Australian art, Australian art and international art. Gallery displays show craft works within the context of other art, allowing visitors opportunities to evaluate contemporary and historical visual art from multiple perspectives. The theories, politics and histories of craft and design are thus interwoven and contrasted with those of other art forms. The representation of contemporary craft and design practice illustrates its technical and cultural heritage and the influence of social, environmental, political and cultural factors.

Robert Bell *Curator Craft and Design*

JAMES A.B. LINTON
born 1904 Perth
died Perth, 1980

Casket
1934
brass with copper and enamel mounts
10 x 27 x 14 cm
purchased with funds from the
Hackett Bequest, 1934

James Linton's father, James W.R. Linton, arrived in Western Australia from England in 1896, quickly establishing a reputation in Perth as an artist, craftsman and teacher. Influential in the development of a number of Perth's first studio crafts practitioners, his work as a metalsmith, jeweller, enamellist and furniture-maker reflected, and popularised in Perth, the style of the late nineteenth-century English Arts and Crafts Movement. James Linton, known as Jamie, studied art at Perth Technical College before joining his father in partnership in 1921. From 1926 to 1927 he also studied in London at the Central School of Arts and Crafts and in Paris with the sculptor Emile-Antoine Bourdelle, before returning to Perth and the family silver-smithing business in 1928. The Lintons' metalwork and jewellery were characterised by simple craftsmanship, rich materials and design imagery derived from study of the local flora. Jamie Linton worked in this style throughout his life, introducing new themes and variations to the Arts and Crafts designs that had been developed by his father. Both are represented in the State Art Collection by a number of works from 1912 to 1955. This casket, made by Jamie Linton, was the first of a number of pieces of the Lintons' work to be acquired by the Art Gallery of Western Australia.

FLORA LANDELLS
born 1888 Adelaide
arrived Perth 1896, active to c1962
died Perth, 1981

Jardiniere
c1933
earthenware, glazed over modelled decoration
51 x 28 x 28 cm
gift of Flora Landells, 1978

Flora Landells commenced working with ceramics in 1912, developing stylised designs of Western Australian and exotic flora for painting on porcelain, a craft for which she gained wide recognition. By about 1925, she had developed an interest in making pottery, pioneering it as a studio craft in Western Australia with the assistance of her husband, Reginald Landells, a chemist. They established the Landells Pottery in Perth, developing unique glazes for use on a range of functional and decorative earthenwareware ceramics.

This large jardiniere, with its design of poinsettia flowers, is typical of Landell's work of the 1930s. Its incised decoration was influenced by a 1909 St Petersberg Imperial Porcelain vase from the Collection; this Landells had admired when visiting the Art Gallery of Western Australia as a child. Her work as an art and ceramic teacher for thirty-five years influenced a generation of artists and established pottery as an art form in Western Australia.

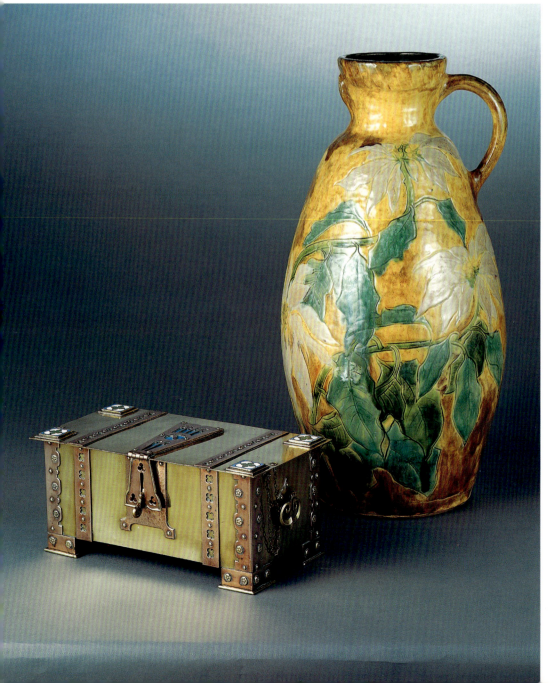

Back cover illustration:

WORCESTER PORCELAIN
established 1751, Worcester, England

'Giles pattern' chestnut basket
c1770
porcelain with overglaze painted decoration
15 x 25 x 21 cm
gift of Dr Harold Schenberg, 1996

Porcelain has been produced in Worcester in England from 1751 to the present. This Worcester porcelain chestnut basket was made during the factory's first period of operation under Dr John Wall, who, with William Davis, developed porcelain manufacture in Britain and forged Worcester's reputation for technical and artistic excellence during England's early industrial period. Durable, translucent and white in colour, porcelain was highly prized for its use in the manufacture of functional and decorative items. This bowl, with its perforated lid and matching stand, is in the decorative style known as Rococo, popular in Europe in the second half of the eighteenth century. Rococo was characterised by its use of fanciful modelled and painted ornamentation derived from natural subjects such as birds, insects and flowers, expressing the elegance of the age. This piece was painted in overglaze enamels in the London workshop of James Giles (1718–1780), an independent decorator who, from 1767 to 1771, painted blank porcelain shapes, supplied by Worcester, with intricate and sumptuous designs.

ST PETERSBURG IMPERIAL PORCELAIN FACTORY
established 1744, St Petersburg, Russia

MARIA KULLER
decorator
Russia

'Maki' vase
1907
porcelain with underglaze pâte-sur-pâte and painted decoration
gift of the Imperial Academy of Sciences, St Petersburg, 1909

The St Petersburg Imperial Porcelain Factory was founded in 1744. As the State factory was closely associated with the Russian Royal Court at St Petersburg, a wide range of highly ornate wares was produced, with modellers and decorators being brought in from other European countries to produce pieces in the current European fashions. During the reign of Tsar Nicholas II (1894–1917), designers and painters from Denmark influenced the production of a range of ceramics in the simpler modern Danish Art Nouveau style popular around 1900–1910.

Using the factory's advanced technical facilities, designers and decorators developed underglaze painting techniques to embody the melancholy mood of Art Nouveau in evocations of the northern Russian landscape. This vase is one of a group of six St Petersburg Imperial Porcelain Factory ceramics in this style that were acquired by the Art Gallery through the Imperial Academy of Sciences in St Petersburg.

EMILE GALLÉ
born 1846 Nancy, France
died Nancy, 1904

'Marine' vase
c1900
cased and etched cameo glass
51 x 24 x 24 cm
gift of Lyn and Kemp Hall, 1994

One of the most influential figures in modern glass-making, Emile Gallé established his workshop in Nancy, France, in 1874. He developed many new decorating techniques for glass which were particularly suited to express the fluid and organic character of the Art Nouveau style popular in Europe at the end of the nineteenth century. Gallé was particularly known for 'cameo' glass, in which designs were etched and engraved through layers of coloured glass.

Exploiting the fluid qualities and intense colours available with glass, Gallé drew on Japanese art and a close observation of the insects and plants of his native Lorraine region to design his work. This vase, one of several in the Collection by Gallé, is typical of his interest in nature, particularly its marine forms. Its sombre colours are intensified by the glass's matte texture and opacity.

DEBORAH COCKS
born 1958 Sydney
lives and works in Tyalgum, New South Wales

Under Sail
1994
glass, slump-formed and enamelled
9 x 58 x 58 cm
purchased 1994

The technical and artistic development of glass has a history of thousands of years, yet contemporary artists working with this material still find new ways to express ideas and emotions through its elusive and seductive qualities. Deborah Cocks is among a number of Australian artists working with glass, using translucent and opaque painted enamels to exploit its particular engagement with light. Painted glass has a long and noble history, yet Cocks uses this technique to invest her glass with a quirky, contemporary humour, in this case as a narrative reflecting on her domestic situation as an artist and a new mother in a rural environment. Her work is part of a particular Australian response to the vibrant international glass movement.

EILEEN KEYS
born 1903 Christchurch, New Zealand
arrived Australia 1947
active in Perth from 1947
died Perth, 1992

Desert
1966
stoneware, partially stained,
46 x 28 x 16 cm
purchased 1966

Eileen Keys was a seminal figure in the development of ceramics in Western Australia, pioneering the use of unusual minerals in the glazing and colouring of her sculptural forms. She commenced ceramics on her arrival in Perth from New Zealand in 1947, deriving design inspiration from Aboriginal art until moving to the production of functional works in the mid-1950s. In these pieces, Eileen Keys adopted an Anglo-Japanese aesthetic as a framework for the expression of the Western Australian landscape through earth-coloured glazes and surface textures. Her more sculptural works of the 1960s, such as Desert, encapsulated the spirit of the period of mineral discovery and development in Western Australia, while providing meditations on the forms of rocks and the bush.

ARTIST UNKNOWN, JAPAN

Inrō with five compartments
c1900
lacquered wood with takamaki-e *decoration*
7 x 6 cm
purchased 1903

Inrō are small personal ornaments used in Japan from the late sixteenth century to the nineteenth century. They took the form of a sectionalised case, with three to five compartments fitted together and held in place by a cord passing through holes at the side of each segment. These were secured by a slip-bead on the cord known as an ojime *and secured on the* obi *(the wide sash of the wearer's garment) by a carved toggle known as a* netsuke. *Inrō were usually made from lacquered wood and intricately decorated, their fine design and craftsmanship conferring status on the wearer. They had a practical use – for carrying seals and medicines – and are today highly prized as examples of Japanese art. This inrō was part of a group of Japanese objects purchased on behalf of the Art Gallery by curators at the Imperial Museum (now the National Museum) in Tokyo in 1903. The group, which includes lacquer, metalwork and ceramics, comprises a fine representation of Japanese crafts of the late Meiji Period.*

AKIO HAMATANI
born 1947 Kyoto, Japan
lives and works in Kyoto

White boat 8
1987
rayon and steel
180 x 550 x 200 cm
purchased 1989

Akio Hamatani is one of a group of Japanese artists who made radical departures in the field of textile and fibre art in the late 1970s. Based in Kyoto and steeped in its ancient and elegant textile traditions, Hamatani uses thread to construct and define large sculptural forms. In the White boat *series, he manipulates the natural parabolic forms of suspended rayon threads to build spacial volumes that interact in dramatic partnership with light and air. The work is at once physical and illusory, echoing the Japanese use of textile in theatre and display and creating an extravagant sense of space with the sparest of means. The boat imagery is alternately revealed and obscured as the viewer moves around the work, its apparent solidity a tantalising paradox created by Hamatani's orchestration of space and narrative.*

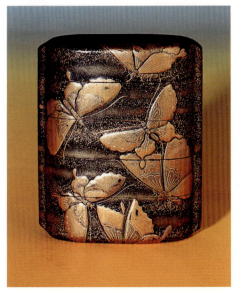

CRAFT AND DESIGN [47]

MICHAEL COOPER
born 1943 Richmond, California, USA
lives and works in Sebastopol, California

Split personality
1982
laminated, turned and carved jarrah on Queensland silver ash base
57 x 126 x 187 cm
purchased with funds from Bunnings Ltd, 1982

The American artist Michael Cooper constructed this work while an Artist-in-Residence at the Art Gallery of Western Australia in 1982. Drawing from sources as diverse as American West Coast hot rod culture, ship model building and vernacular woodcraft traditions, Cooper's work is a tour de force of craftsmanship and illusion. In a commentary on violence, the central body shape of the motorcycle is formed as a gun, rendered powerless through being constructed in wood, while the cycle itself is reduced to a model-like scale. He thus interchanges images of home-based and community-based traditions of woodcraft and toys. Cooper used innovative technology for moulding laminated veneers of Western Australian jarrah to construct the curvilinear elements of the work and wood-turning techniques for its hundreds of other elements. The surreal, boat-shaped sidecar was influenced by the traditional shipbuilding environment of Fremantle, the location of Cooper's influential three-month residency in Western Australia.

CHRISTOPHER ROBERTSON
born 1957, Norseman, Western Australia
active in Perth to 1997
lives and works in Canberra

Chair
1983
jarrah and wandoo
86 x 73 x 99 cm
purchased 1988

Christopher Robertson was born and trained in Western Australia both as a jeweller/metalsmith and a furniture designer/maker. His work reflects a passionate interest in the forms and growth structures of Australian plants, using native timbers in dramatic combinations with other materials. His concern for function is expressed in this rocking chair, its utility in harmony with its strong graphic presence. The main timber used is jarrah, native to the south-western region of Western Australia and used in the State since the early nineteenth century for furniture and construction. In this chair the strict geometry and plain surfaces traditionally associated with the use of jarrah are contrasted with an informal structural element of wandoo, another native timber with a figured grain revealed through Robertson's craftsmanship.

ROGER FRY
designer
born 1866, London, England
died London, 1934

JOSEPH KALLENBORN & SONS
manufacturer
London

Table
1913
holly with marquetry veneer decoration
70 x 72 x 72 cm
purchased with funds from the
Audrey Priscilla Jenkin Bequest, 1996

This table was designed by the British artist and theorist Roger Fry for the Omega Workshops in London. The Workshops were set up by Fry in 1913 to produce a range of Modernist household objects designed by artists associated with the Bloomsbury School. Omega objects were characterised by their highly coloured abstract decoration and were produced by young artists interested in modern design and Post-Impressionism. The bold shapes interpreted in fine wood marquetry veneers on this small table were typical of Fry's approach to design. The table was part of a small range of furniture produced in limited numbers to Fry's designs by the English cabinetmaker Joseph Kallenborn & Sons. It was an alternative to the mainstream furniture of the period and a precursor to the angular, geometric design popularised in the 1920s. This table illustrates the period of influence of British formalist Modernism on Australian Modernist artists of the early twentieth century.

MARGARET WEST
born 1936 Melbourne
lives and works in Sydney

Seven caskets for red sand (recapitulation)
1987
granite and Carrara marble, incised,
lined with lead and filled with red desert sand
each casket 67 x 7 x 7 cm
purchased 1987

Margaret West's work explores the metaphysical, psychological and social aspects of jewellery and small personal objects. This set of small marble and granite caskets alludes to the tradition of the jewellery box and its contents of precious stones and metals. Like ancient sarcophagi, they use stone to encapsulate and preserve fragile materials and fleeting memories. In this group, West uses measured portions of red desert sand to concentrate the vision and humanise the scale of the Australian landscape. The caskets are lined with lead, a material both protective and destructive, to further distil the experience of the material and remind the viewer of the inevitable transience of life.

HENNING KOPPEL
designer
born 1918 Copenhagen, Denmark
died Copenhagen, 1981

GEORG JENSEN SØLVSMEDIE
maker
established 1904 Copenhagen, Denmark

Pitcher
design 1952, manufacture c1967
sterling silver
42 x 24 x 15 cm
purchased 1968

The Danish silversmithing firm of Georg Jensen was founded in Copenhagen in 1904. Jensen was one of the most innovative designers of the period, producing a range of jewellery and objects in a restrained and simple style. Throughout the twentieth century, the firm engaged many innovative silversmiths and designers, among them Henning Koppel. His work for Georg Jensen from the late 1940s encapsulated the sculptural and organic design sensibilities of the mid-century period. It was among the finest expressions of Scandinavian design, using fluid, unadorned forms to emphasise the subtle colour and reflective qualities of silver. Koppel also worked for other Danish companies, designing objects in materials such as ceramics and plastics. One of Koppel's most famous designs, this water pitcher placed him at the forefront of European mid-century Modernism. It is part of the Gallery's collection of Scandinavian craft and design objects of the 1950s and 1960s, the period of its greatest international influence.

HANS COPER
born 1920 Chemnitz, Germany
arrived England 1939
lived and worked in London and Frome
died London, 1981

Round bodied vase
c1967
glazed stoneware
21 x 18 x 16 cm
purchased 1984

and
LUCIE RIE
born 1902 Vienna, Austria
arrived England 1938
lived and worked in London
died London, 1995

Bottle vase
c1967
glazed stoneware
32 x 18 x 18 cm
purchased 1984

Lucie Rie and Hans Coper both emigrated to Britain just prior to the onset of World War II and worked together for twelve years from 1946 at Rie's studio in London. Both artists brought a new dimension to British studio ceramics, connecting it to modern European sculpture and historical Chinese and Mediterranean ceramics and influencing a generation of potters in the 1950s and 1960s. Lucie Rie had trained in Vienna in the 1920s, and her ceramics reflected the elegant and refined modernity of that period of Austrian design. During a long and distinguished career in England, she developed a range of functional ceramics notable for their use of subtle glazes on sculptural, organic forms. Hans Coper also used the vessel form as a point of reference in his abstract compositions. Like Lucie Rie, he used a limited range of basic forms to draw attention to the subtleties of his textured glazes and surfaces and his precise technical methods to develop the distinctive spacial relationships in his work.

Contemporary Art

One of the most striking aspects of the history of contemporary art in the State Art Collection is that its scale and ambition closely parallel the Gallery's desire and ability to play a key role in the cultural life of Western Australians. While the growth of this part of the Collection from the early 1960s to the late 1990s reflects the Gallery's increased independence and resources, its character equally reflects the expanding field of ideas and materials that artists have been working with through this period.

The Perth Prize for Contemporary Art, initiated in 1954, continued as an important annual event in the exhibition schedule into the 1960s, a broad range of Western Australian artists being seen alongside their colleagues from the eastern States. The exhibition gave rise to much debate and was an important source of acquisitions. By the mid-1960s the event had been transformed into the Perth Prize for Drawing, which became an important source of international acquisitions. Jim Dine's *The cellist* is one such example. A beautifully rendered charcoal drawing, this work later was the source for *The cellist against blue*, one of *Eight sheets from an undefined novel*, an important suite of Dine's prints.

The purchase of Henry Moore's *Reclining figure* in 1963 again sparked off a local debate about the Modernist sculptor's abstraction of the human figure. Such a debate was neither new nor specific to Perth, yet what is clear is that it raised the public's interest in contemporary art and set a new level of ambition for the kind of work that might be acquired. The Gallery's ability to attract donations and acquire works of art increased dramatically with the announcement in 1967 of the development of a Cultural Centre for Perth which was to include a new art gallery. The ambitions signalled by the purchase of the Henry Moore sculpture began to appear as an achievable goal.

As the work of numerous Western Australian artists continued to be acquired alongside increased international purchases, the State Art Collection began to achieve the breadth of focus essential for exploring the many ways in which art from Western Australia is linked to art from other places around the world. The purchase of modern and contemporary art has enabled the Gallery to build a collection of increasing international significance. It has, for example, a significant collection of modern British works, including paintings by Stanley Spencer, Ben Nicholson, Frank Auerbach and Lucian Freud.

During the 1980s and 1990s the Gallery has continued to purchase contemporary works of art. There is an extensive collection of art from Western Australia but, importantly, this is seen in an increasingly broad and dynamic context. Contemporary artists work in a wide range of media with an enormous diversity of ideas and across many social and cultural contexts. Over the last forty years not only has there been an expansion in the range of media but in the way they are combined and recombined. This expanded field of material possibilities, and the diverse cultural and social reference points available to the artist, create new challenges and possibilities for the Art Gallery.

The collection includes several works by Carol Rudyard, which are significant reflections on the way in which literary and art historical sources might co-exist with and be invigorated by materials and objects that we experience in our daily lives. Acquisitions of important works by Ian Burn and Robert MacPherson, which explore the possibilities and limitations of everyday experience, perhaps best exemplify the poles of anguished doubt and playful possibility made possible in contemporary artistic practice.

Trevor Smith *Curator Contemporary Art*

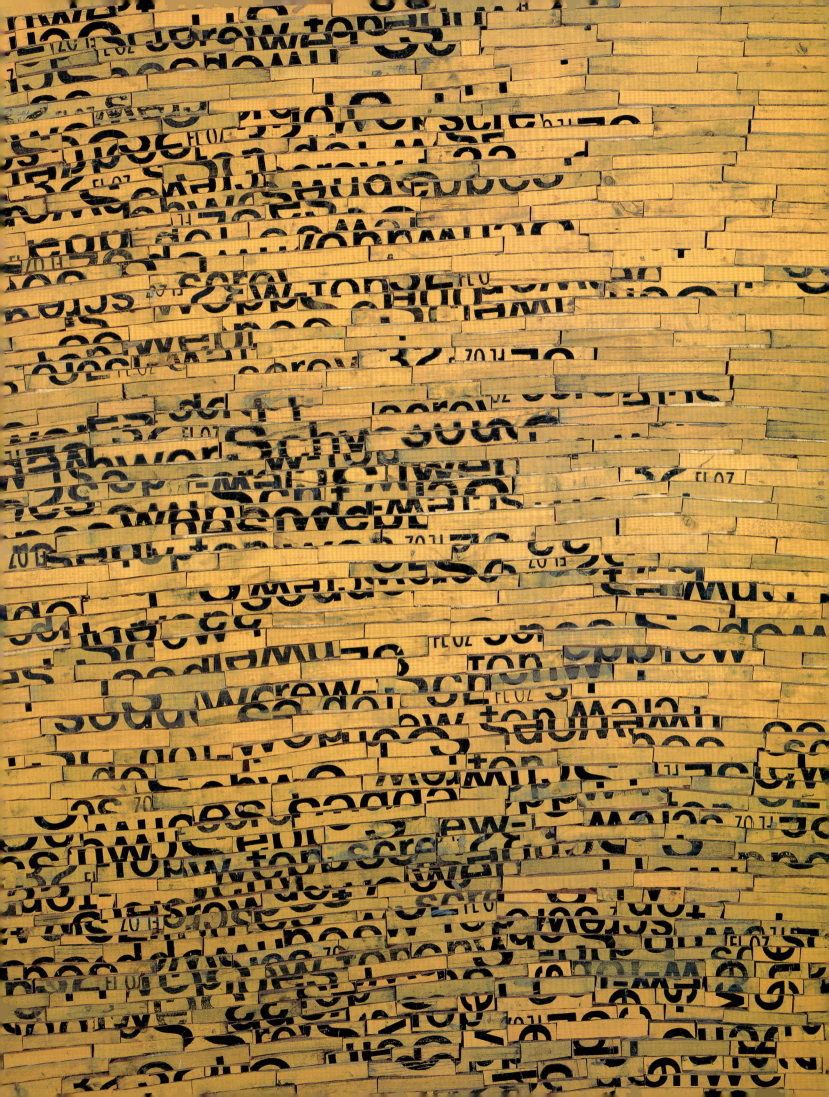

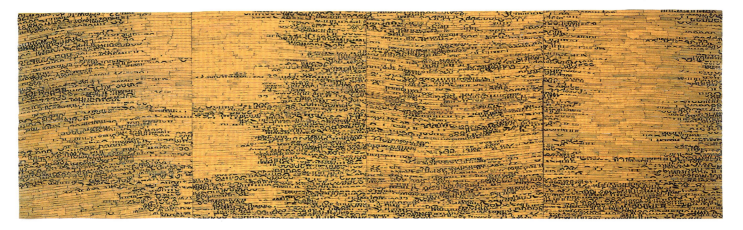

ROSALIE GASCOIGNE
born 1917 Auckland, New Zealand
arrived Australia 1943
lives and works in Canberra

Monaro
1989
sawn and split soft drink crates on plywood
four panels, 131 x 457 cm overall
purchased 1989
(© Copyright 1989 Rosalie Gascoigne. Reproduced by permission of VI$COPY Ltd, 1997)

Materials that both mark the landscape and have been marked by it – road signs, wooden soft drink cases, old linoleum, weathered enamelware – these are the raw materials of Rosalie Gascoigne's art. She transforms humble signs of human presence in the landscape into constructions and installations which lyrically evoke her affinity for the landscape outside her home in Canberra. Monaro is a reference to the Monaro plains, south-east of Canberra, near Cooma.

By splitting, sawing and recombining wooden Schweppes soft drink crates, Gascoigne creates a powerfully undulating field of yellow and black which cascades across four large panels. Rhythmically manipulating the black lettering into patterns, Gascoigne evokes wind rippling through wheat fields or subtle variations in the fall of the land under moving shadows. As Anne Kirker has noted, '. . . the black text flows rhythmically through a golden matrix commemorating a landscape of human use rather than untouched nature'. *

* Anne Kirker, 'Art that calls us into relationship: a way of interpreting McCahon and Gascoigne,' *Rosalie Gascoigne Colin McCahon: Sense of Place* (catalogue), Sydney, Ivan Doughterty Gallery, 1990, p. 21.

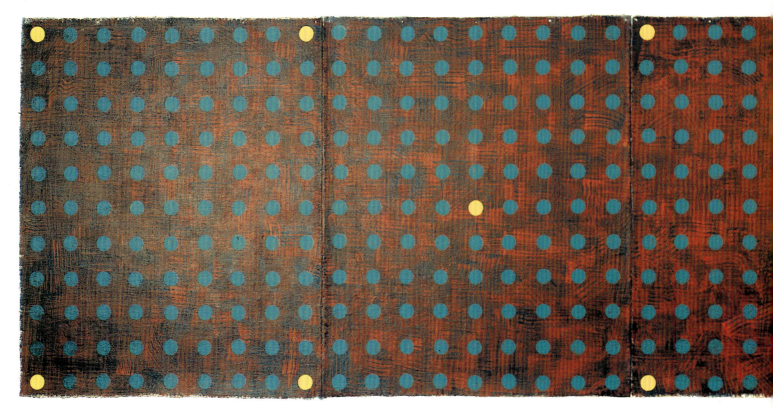

BRIAN BLANCHFLOWER
born 1939 Brighton, England
arrived Australia 1972
lives and works in Perth

Canopy XXXII 'Ninety-nine days'
1993
synthetic polymer on laminated hessian
five elements, 225 x 930 cm overall
purchased 1996

Brian Blanchflower is recognised as one of Australia's foremost painters, and the Canopy series, begun in 1985 is one of his most important accomplishments. As he has stated, 'I moved away from dealing with land surface and concentrated almost entirely on a view out on the universe, which is what all the Canopies are about. It's about what you can see in the sky. Obviously, as you're looking out you're seeing that things are reflected in yourself.' *

These are large paintings, Canopy XXXII 'Ninety-nine days' being over nine metres long. Laid across five panels, a grid of blue discs hovers against a scumbled red ground, yellow disks alternately marking the centres and the extremities of each of the individual panels. Where his earlier work tended to use more organic materials and colouration in order to evoke particular experiences in the landscape, Canopy XXXII is carefully built up out of near primary colours and is an excellent example of Blanchflower's use of rigorous formal structures.

* Brian Blanchflower in 'An Interview with Brian Blanchflower: David Bromfield', *Brian Blanchflower Works 1961–1989*, Perth, Department of Fine Arts, University of Western Australia, 1989.

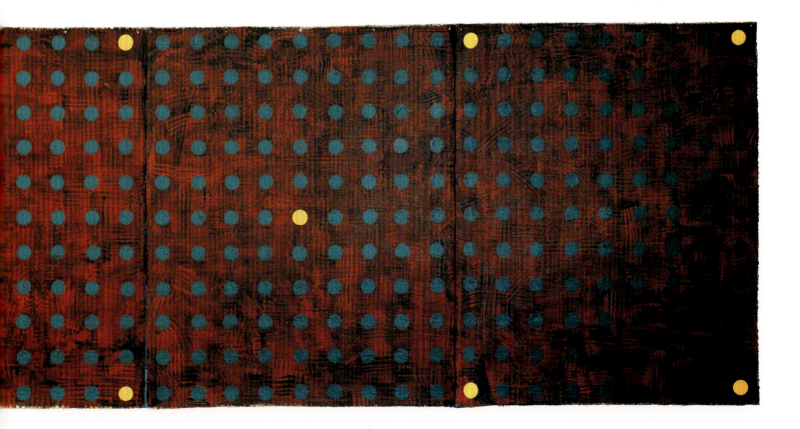

CONTEMPORARY ART   [55]

KEN UNSWORTH
born 1931 Melbourne
lives and works in Sydney

Suspended stone circle
1978–1981
river stones, black annealed wire and steel
255 cm diameter
purchased 1982

Ken Unsworth's Suspended stone circle is from a group of works that he produced using river stones that he collected himself and arranged in suspension formations. Similar work was exhibited at the Venice Biennale in 1978, and this particular piece was installed in the Sculpture Triennale in Melbourne and at an exhibition entitled 'Construction in Process in the Art of the Seventies' in Lodz, Poland, in 1981. Suspended stone circle is simple in form but stunning in its visual impact. River stones forming a large ring, two and a half metres in diameter, are suspended from poles and hover just off the ground. Material that has been smoothed and shaped by the course of time is arranged in classic geometric formation, and the wires suspending the stones create a drawing in space and delicately poise the work between the mundane and the magical.

HOWARD TAYLOR
born 1918 Hamilton, Victoria
arrived Western Australia 1932
lives and works in Northcliffe,
Western Australia

Light source reverse
1994
synthetic polymer and oil on wood
209 x 209 x 9 cm
purchased with funds from the
Sir Claude Hotchin Art Foundation, 1995

Howard Taylor is one of Australia's most significant artists. The land affected by the phenomena of light and weather has been the single unifying factor in the work he has produced over six decades. His acute observation of the Western Australian bush, in combination with unrelenting experimentation, has allowed him to create a personal style and approach. Taylor's observations of this unique landscape reach an astonishing summation in Light source reverse. The theme of sun/sphere is emblematic of his explorations of light, perception and form. His works seek to reconcile the almost imperceptible nuances in the landscape by focusing on the processes of differentiation central to human perception.

CONTEMPORARY ART [57]

SUSAN NORRIE
born 1953 Sydney
lives and works in Sydney

Error of closure
1994
lacquered stand and shelf, glass, rubber stamp, pencil, wood, light box, photoscan on canvas
dimensions variable
purchased 1996

Error of closure is a pivotal work in Susan Norrie's practice and one of her most ambitious works to date. Typically this installation demonstrates her fondness for the Surrealist mode of juxtaposition and contrast, creating an unsettling dialogue between sources and media that have historically been characterised as separate and different. She works between media (painting, sculpture, photography and the 'readymade') and art historical sources (Albrecht Durer, Andre Breton, Louis Sullivan, Marcel Duchamp and Jean-Baptiste Chardin), the associations invoked by any one component being activated only through the relationship with the other objects in the ensemble. It is through this dynamic interaction that Error of closure *meditates on surface, lightness, chance and mortality. It is as if the blindfolded woman in the Chardin stands in for Norrie herself, conjuring up the complex and uncanny web of connections marking her place in the world.*

[58]   ART GALLERY OF WESTERN AUSTRALIA

CAROL RUDYARD
born 1922 England
arrived Australia 1950
lives and works in Perth

Salt cellar and glass
1988
mixed media video installation
dimensions variable
purchased 1988

Balanced between precise historical allusion and poetic play, Carol Rudyard's installations examine and re-animate concerns of early Modernist painters and poets, who found in the simplest of everyday occurrences the grandest of poetic possibilities. Salt cellar and glass is, in part, a poem to Marcel Duchamp, the artist who first deployed the readymade (the nomination of an 'ordinary' object as a work of art). While Rudyard's own choice of readymades is laden with allusions to Duchamp, they are also, like those employed by Duchamp in the second decade of this century, commonplace objects: a mirror, artificial flowers and pot plants, cocktail glasses, a table lamp, a television, modern furniture and floor tiles. These objects are placed amongst modular white blocks which look like museum furniture but also mark out the boundaries of the domestic tableau. Salt cellar and glass sets out a space of contemplation, allowing us to look at the overlooked.

CONTEMPORARY ART   [59]

MIRIAM STANNAGE
born 1939 Northam, Western Australia
lives and works in Perth

Watergate
1973–74
*felt-tipped pen and lead pencil
on synthetic polymer on canvas*
147 x 229 cm
purchased 1989

Like that of many contemporary artists, Miriam Stannage's work is characterised less by the use of a particular medium or technique than by a focus on a set of issues or ideas. Perception in both the physical and social senses of the term is the lynchpin around which her explorations revolve. Watergate is one of an important series of canvases from the 1970s whose surfaces were cross-hatched with texts drawn from the news of the day or the history of art. Watergate, of course, refers to the scandal which caused the downfall of US President Richard Nixon.

While Watergate's text forms a grid which is coextensive with the entire surface of the canvas, almost in a parody of Modernist painting, the way the lines of writing cross each other at ninety degrees also refers back to early forms of colonial correspondence, where one letter would be overwritten by another in order to save on precious paper. The irony of contemporary news events broadcast around the globe transcribed in a technique of writing originally utilised to deal with conditions of extreme isolation cannot be overlooked, and must be seen as a critical meditation on the information explosion that is increasingly dominating our lives.

ROBERT MACPHERSON
born 1937 Brisbane
lives and works in Brisbane

Mayfair: Thirty five paintings, thirty five signs in memory of G.W. and Reno Castelli
1993–1994
synthetic polymer on hardboard and plywood
35 panels, each 61 x 91 cm (variable)
purchased with funds from the
Sir Claude Hotchin Art Foundation, 1995

This work continues Robert MacPherson's interest in the strata of language in our daily experience. His dismay at the loss of languages and the richness of culturally specific vocabularies has led him to build works of art around vocabularies as diverse as Latin classificatory systems and the languages of metholated spirits drinkers, the disappearing working class, fishermen and children.

In this work, his focus is roadside sign painting techniques and the coded language used by Holden aficionados in advertising. These expressions, only meaningful to insiders, make a comment often made about the language of art criticism. While drawing upon roadside signs, the arrangements of colour, the bedrock of all MacPherson's work, are particularly evident.

BRIAN McKAY
born 1926 Meckering, Western Australia
lives and works in Fremantle

Blue recess II
1974
oil on canvas
120 x 120 cm
gift of Sue and Ian Bernadt, 1994

From highly textured canvases evocative of the weathering effects of time to the immediacy of Hard-Edged geometric abstractions, Brian McKay has pursued a singular path. One of a number of works painted on his return from Greece and London, Blue recess is an example of the more reductive, Hard-Edged area of his practice. In typical modernist fashion, the painting is structured as a series of repetitions of the shape of the canvas, in this instance placed at an angle to its edges. This rectangle then generates a series of triangles and other rectangles painted in varying shades and tones of blue. Luceille Hanley has observed that blue is a predominant colour in McKay's practice, a fact that the artist suggests may have to do with the multi-hued blue sky and sea of Western Australia and to the pacifist principles often associated with that colour.*

* Luceille Hanley, 'Man and maker' in *Brian McKay: Painter*, Fremantle, Fremantle Arts Centre Press, 1991, p. 53

CONTEMPORARY ART [61]

LEON GOLUB
born 1922 Chicago, USA
lives and works in New York City

White Squad III
1982
synthetic polymer on canvas
305 x 437 cm
purchased with funds provided by the
Art Gallery of Western Australia Foundation,
1997

For the past five decades Leon Golub has maintained an intense commitment to figurative representation and emotionally charged subjects which reveal human existence in crisis. Golub's paintings are often contradictory, with a rich and vigorously worked surface of harmonic colour in uncomfortable proximity to violent events and 'real' people.

In the White Squad series he combines figures drawn from diverse sources such as press photos from China in the 1920s and news images of American police and sports personalities to articulate a rage against individual acts of violence. Golub does not withdraw from ugly situations but instead, through scale and eye contact, he positions us, if not as accessories, at least as psychologically compromised participants.

The head, always central to Golub's imagery as a metaphor for the intellect and the imagination, becomes in the White Squad paintings the point of mediation between one figure's power and the other's vulnerability. He has defined the role of painting, and contemporary history painting in particular, as bearing witness. We are witnesses to the raw intensity of Golub's subjects in paintings which question how we shift responsibility to others elsewhere.

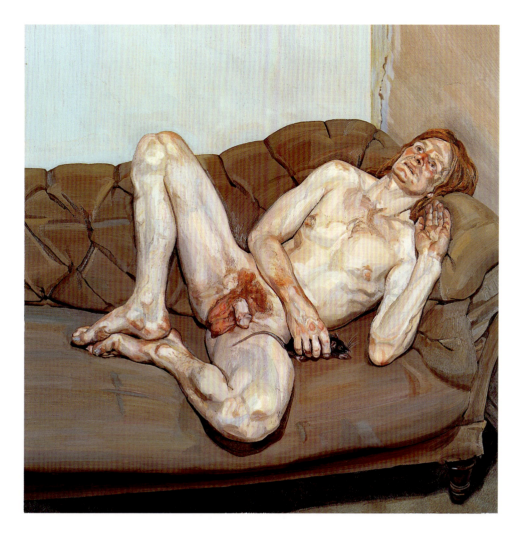

Front cover illustration:

JOHN DE ANDREA
born 1941 Denver, USA
lives and works in Denver

Allegory: after Courbet
1988
oil on polyvinyl and mixed media
172 x 152 x 190 cm
purchased 1989

Allegory: after Courbet by John de Andrea is an excellent example of the work of this leading exponent of New Realist sculpture. The work is one of a small number of self-portraits executed by the artist, and it places him in dialogue with one of the central figures of Realism in the nineteenth century: Gustav Courbet. Inspired by Courbet's Interior of my studio, a real allegory summing up seven years of my life as an artist, de Andrea's sculpture focuses in on the central pairing of artist and model (or muse), which is rather dwarfed by the sprawling array of friends, associates and hangers-on that Courbet chose to work into his massive canvas. As an allegory of the artist's practice, it is a rather more contained one than that suggested by Courbet, and perhaps it is implicitly critical of the social overtones in the latter work. The neutral colouring of the tableau would also seem to suggest a desire to hold the work at a distance from the flux of everyday experience, drawing its power from the gap between reality observed and its representation.

LUCIAN FREUD
born 1922 Berlin
arrived England 1933
lives and works in London

Naked man with rat
1977–78
oil on canvas
92 x 91 cm
purchased 1984

Renowned for his ability to make paint stand for flesh, Lucian Freud has found an almost exclusive focus in the human form. Naked man with rat is an excellent example of his work of the late 1970s, its lush painterly quality both underscoring and distancing the unsettling pose of the sitter. There is a taut intensity to the painted figure, the scumbled brushwork standing in relief against the dark surfaces of the couch. This effect amplifies Freud's sinuous line, which draws the eye around the body, concentrating our attention more on its extremities – its awkwardly splayed legs, open left hand, eyes staring up into space – than on the rat alluded to in the title or the flaccid penis, which lies virtually at the centre of the composition.

At the time of its purchase in 1984 there was some concern over the gender and pose of the sitter, yet in retrospect Naked man with rat has proved to have been one of the Gallery's most important purchases, widely exhibited internationally and achieving recognition as a major work by one of the great figurative painters of the twentieth century.

CONTEMPORARY ART [63]

ROBERT JUNIPER
born 1929 Merredin, Western Australia
lives and works in Darlington, Western Australia

Outcamp
1977
oil on canvas
173 x 234 cm
purchased with the assistance of the Friends of the Art Gallery of Western Australia, 1978

Since the 1960s Robert Juniper has been a key figure in contemporary Australian painting. His primary subject has been human interaction with the often forbidding landscape of Western Australia. Outcamp is an excellent example of Juniper's work from the period. A densely textured ground is built up from colours redolent of the desert landscape and superimposed by symbolic and geometric markings. In their stark contrast of surface and geometry, these markings evoke the human impact on the landscape. Elwyn Lynn has written that 'Juniper had painted "Outcamp" as if there could be no kinship between objects in the desert; the houses, old walls, probably shop signs, bits of iron and housing timbers are scattered as if by a cyclone, but much of this dispersal is due to cannibalisation; what might be useful is taken elsewhere and such towns gradually disappear.' *

*Elwyn Lynn, The Art of Robert Juniper, Sydney, Craftsman House, 1986, p. 23

[64] ART GALLERY OF WESTERN AUSTRALIA